Preparing for the Bridegroom

Preparing for the Bridegroom

Rehearsal

MICHELE M. GAYLE

AuthorHouse™ LLC
1663 Liberty Drive
Bloomington, IN 47403
www.authorhouse.com
Phone: 1-800-839-8640

Published by AuthorHouse 05/13/2014

ISBN: 978-1-4918-7188-1 (sc)
ISBN: 978-1-4918-7187-4 (e)

Library of Congress Control Number: 2014904562

A notice of Copyright:

To the memory of my beloved mother

Rev. Dr. Cynthia L. Miller.

You are not forgotten. You live on in who I am, and is becoming.

Dedication

This book is dedicated to the Bride of Yeshua Ministries Inc. May all who read this book know the truth and be set free.

Contents

Preface

This book is directly inspired by a vision I saw. I believe the Lord's intentions for this study is to awake the consciousness of the Church to be ready for Christ coming, which is indeed quite eminent. And also to reveal the truth as it relates to our responsibility to up-hold holy worship unto God. That the holy observances become for us as He had ordained and commanded in the Old Testament; fulfilled, substantiated and upheld by our Lord Yeshua [Jesus] as recorded in the New Testament.

Introduction

The Lord Jesus will return, this is His promise in St. John chapter fourteen *"For I go to prepare a place for you and if I go I will come again to receive you unto myself that where I am there ye may be also."* (Jn.14:2c, 3)

This Pledge Messiah intended to serve as comfort to the disciples and believers of the early church and to us today. There was no need to be troubled, anxious and full of fear because of His departure. He assured them and us that He will come again. He was leaving on account of us.

One, it is to prepare a home for us with Him. Second, it is that the Holy Spirit will come to us as promised before, by the Father. (Acts 1:4)

Even this in its self should serve to our comfort—we are not alone, not abandon and not forsaken! We have the promise and seal.

There is however something very intriguing here in this text. I am referring to the above mentioned verse from John chapter 14. This scripture verse is better understood by the Lord Jesus' Jewish audience of His day, than it does to us today. We, in our twenty-first Century Western Civilized Culture will not readily note all that is being implied by the Lord Jesus. In order for us to fully comprehend what Christ was really saying and what the people of His day understood Him to have said, it is necessary for us to become familiarized with the Ancient Jewish Customs. We must especially have some understanding of the Ancient Jewish Wedding. In fact, this promise, "Behold I go to prepare a place for you and I will come again to receive you unto myself . . ." was made by the Lord Jesus, and is almost a direct quote from the vow that a groom would have spoken to his bride during their betrothal ceremony.

So in part one of this book we are going to be looking at the "Ancient Jewish wedding" and how it parallels the Lord Jesus and the Church.

Having accomplished my task, we will then have a grasp; a better understanding of who we truly are in Christ Jesus. Not only that, but we will definitely know what is expected of us as we await His return.

Part 1

Yeshua and His Bride in Ancient Jewish Wedding

Shiddukin — Choosing of the Bride

It is the very wise king Solomon who said "Whoever finds a wife finds a good thing, and obtains favor of the LORD. (Prov.18:22) Today in our western culture it seems very normative for men and women to just have a good time with no strings attached. It is completely acceptable to live together outside of Holy matrimony (Marriage). Some appear to be contented and totally resigned to living void of any marital commitment—a let the chips fall where they may sort of attitude.

The wedding or marriage as instituted by God in the Book of Genesis is for most old fashion and to some point nonexistent. Even among those of faith there appears to be a general disregard for this scriptural or biblical requirement. Also, with civil laws favoring common law and same sex unions we have in deed strayed very far from the biblical plan for Marriage. As a result of how far our society has gone away from this divinely instituted act, we are unable to truly understand in context what the bible is saying when it uses illustrations involving marriages.

Our concept of marriage is very significantly different to that of the Holy Bible and the Ancient Hebrew marriage customs.

In Biblical times it was that, a man having found a wife; seeing a woman that is deemed wife material. One the man considers to be well pleasing to him; the order of that day was, he would approach his parents about the matter; asking that they, or his father should secure the potential Bride for him.

This was what Samson did. Remember how he insisted on his parents for the philistine woman. *"Get her for me; for she pleaseth me well."* Then they went down with him to do the business of acquiring the Bride. (Judges 14: 3)

However there is yet a stricter practice that I prefer to use here as an example for the first stage of this marriage process. It is that of the father being the one with the responsibility to find a wife for his son. The father being aware; having full knowledge of his son's measure of maturity and his need for a wife. He planned for his son's marriage. He looked for a wife and when he had seen such worthy candidate, he approached her and her family with his intentions.

This Stage is called the Shiddukhin—this was the first necessary step of arrangements preliminary to the Betrothal.

The father of the groom was the one with the responsibility to find and secure a wife for His son. I'll use for my example, Abraham and his son Isaac (Gen. 24:1-4). However Abraham being old in age was physically unable to personally fulfill his role as the one having the responsibility of finding his son a wife. Therefore the great task he conferred by oath upon someone else. He appointed his chief servant to act as a broker on his behalf. This person fulfilled his role in a manner that completely satisfied all the wishes and stipulations of Isaac's father with exactness.

So it is also for Christ Jesus and the Church, that God the Father chose the Bride for His Son.

In the Old Testament the LORD is regarded as the Bride Groom of Israel, In the New Testament Jesus as the Bridegroom of the Church.

Deuteronomy chapter seven and verse six states, *"For thou art an holy people unto the LORD thy God: the LORD thy God hath chosen thee to be a special people unto himself, above all people that are upon the face of the earth."* Also *"For your husband is your Maker . . ."*

(Is. 54:5-6)

The beautiful thing in the comparison of Christ and the church, is that here, the father of the Groom is also the Father who stands to represent the Bride as well. She is His, He loves her—it is a perfect match made by God the Father in Heaven, it is all His doing—His initiative! Listen to the heart of this text by the Apostle Paul's letter to the Ephesians. *"Husbands love your wives, just as Christ loved the church and gave himself up for her to make her holy. Cleansing her by the washing with water through the word. And* **to present her to himself as a radiant church.** *Without stain or wrinkle or any other blemish, but holy and blameless. In the same way, husbands ought to love their wives as their own bodies. He who loves his wife loves himself. After all, no one ever hated his own body, but he feeds and cares for it, just as Christ does the church —* **but I am talking about Christ and the church."** (Eph. 5:25-32)

"For he chose us in him before the creation of the world to be holy and blameless in his sight." Says Ephesians chapter one and verses four. We are His!

Time and time again through out the scriptures is this beautiful comparison of a marriage drawn. God has so intricately woven through the pages of the canon; revealed through the Antiquity of the Jews, this marvelous illustration of a Bride and Bridegroom. This He used to reveal and to teach us of this special love relationship between Him and His people or Christ Jesus and His Church.

The Lord Jesus was asked this question, "why do not your disciples fast as do John's disciple?" he answered them saying,

"While the bridegroom is with them, the attendants of the bride do not fast, do they? So long as they have the bridegroom with them, they cannot fast. But the days will come when the bridegroom is taken away from them, and then they will fast in that day." (Mk. 2:19-20)

Another example is also found in John chapter three and verses twenty seven to twenty nine, *John answered and said, A man can receive nothing, except it be given him from heaven. Ye yourselves bear me witness, that I said, I am not the Messiah, but that I am sent before Him. He that hath the bride is the bridegroom: but the friend of the bridegroom, which standeth and heareth him, rejoiceth greatly because of the bridegroom's voice: this my joy therefore is fulfilled.*

Apostle Paul uses the example of Christ and the church to illustrate how the relationship of husbands and wives aught to be.

"For the husband is the head of the wife, as Christ also is the head of the church, He Himself being the Savior of the body."(Eph.5:23)

We, (All Saints) are the chosen bride of Christ Jesus. God the Father has with perfect delight chosen us to be the precious Bride of His Beloved Son. These were the words spoken to Israel in Exodus chapter 19 verses 5 to 6: "Now therefore, if you will indeed obey my voice and keep my covenant, you shall be my treasured possession among all peoples, for all peoples, for all the earth is mine; and you shall be to me a kingdom of priests and a holy nation. These are the words that you shall speak to the people of Israel. "Later on apostle Peter spoke similarly to the New Testament Church saying," But ye are a chosen generation, a royal priesthood, an holy nation, a peculiar people; that ye should shew forth the praises of him who hath called you out of darkness into his marvelous light;"

The heavenly Father is still working the same plan—the plan he had from the very beginning—uniting all, making twain one, in the body of Christ Jesus.

So even as Abraham had chosen and assigned an agent or broker to act on his behalf in choosing a wife for Isaac his beloved son, so it is also that God the Father sends the Holy Spirit as the broker to find the Bride for His beloved Son. The Holy Spirit accomplishes this in us through the conviction of sin, which causes us to acknowledge our need of Christ our Savior: Galatians chapter four and verse six: ". . . God has sent forth the Spirit of His Son into our hearts . . ."

". . . for the Spirit searches all things, even the depths of God." (1Cor. 2:10)

This is what the Lord said in regards to the coming of the Holy Spirit and the work He will accomplish:

"Nevertheless I tell you the truth; It is expedient for you that I go away: for if I go not away, the Comforter will not come unto you; but if I depart, I will send him unto you."

And when he is come, he will reprove the world of sin, and of righteousness, and of judgment:" (Jn. 16:7, 8)

The Lord Jesus said, no one comes to me except by the Father who sent me. (Jn. 6:44)

God's people are chosen, according to John chapter fifteen and verse sixteen, which states: *"Ye have not chosen me, but **I have chosen you**, and ordained you . . ."* said the Lord Jesus.

Also, 2 Thessalonians chapter 2 and verse 13 *"God hath from the beginning chosen you to salvation through sanctification of the Spirit and belief of the truth"* Holy Spirit is God's agent of choice who chooses, draws and woo His Bride and also sanctifies—sets her apart for Him.

It is entirely the work of the Heavenly Father. Listen to a statement made by our Lord Jesus, *"I can do nothing on My own initiative . . . I do not seek My own will, but the will of Him who sent Me." (Jn. 5:30)*

I love 1 Peter chapter 1 and verse 8. It does bears a striking similarity between Christ and His bride and Isaac and the bride that was chosen for him. Isaac had not seen his bride neither had she seen her groom which she had committed to love. Not until she was brought to him in his country by the broker the chief servant of Abraham his father. When her eyes lighted on him she loved him from the start and it was the same for him, a love at first sight! *"And though you have not seen Him, you love Him, and though you do not see Him now, but believe in Him, you greatly rejoice with joy inexpressible and full of glory.* Having not seen we love him, our Lord and King and by faith in Him we rejoice at His glorious appearing! We wait with great expectancy for Him, knowing that He will come for us as He had promised. As He had promised so we believe and anticipate this glorious manifestation; when we shall behold Him face to face, even as He is. I imagine He will show us the scars from the nails which was hammered through His hands. We will see His scarred feet, the evidences of the price He paid to purchase us for Himself.

This brings us now to the next stage which is called the Ketubah.

Ketubah—The Contract

The stage of determining the suited Bride is completed. The Groom and His father or the Groom's father or agent has made the necessary preliminaries thus far, but like in everything else we want some guarantees, so a contract is made. In the contract are the stipulations and conditions for the Marriage. Mainly it is the Bride's price, the commitment of the Groom to support and to provide for his Bride and the bride she declares her dowry and her willingness to be his on the conditions that have been set forth.

The latter however seemed to not have always been the case necessarily. It does not appear that in all situations the consent or approval of the bride was required.

There are very specific obligations the husband must perform, as is set out in Exodus chapter 21 and verse 10. He has the responsibility to provide his wife with her food, her clothing, and her conjugal rights. It is from the apocryphal Tobit (7:14) that we find a direct reference to a Ketubah or marriage contract.

(Yamauchi, 246.)

Tobit 7:12-16 it says, "Raguel called for his daughter Sarah, took her by the hand and gave her to Tobias with these words, `I entrust her to you; the law and the ruling recorded in the Book of Moses assign her to you as your wife. Take her; take her home to your father's house with a good conscience. The God of heaven grant you a good journey in peace.' Then he turned to her mother and asked her to fetch him writing paper. He drew up the marriage contract, how he gave his daughter as bride to Tobias according to the ordinance in the Law of Moses.

I have gleaned quite a bit of knowledge on this subject from *Bill Risk's Ancient Jewish Marriage traditions.* Richard Booker, *Here Comes The Bride: Jewish Wedding Customs And The Messiah*, (Houston: Sounds of the Trumpet, 1995), 4-5. I credit my knowledge and information on this particular subject to them.

Please recall that the ketubah is the written specifications of the bride price, the promises of the Groom, and the rights of the bride. In the Old Testament, Israel is viewed as the bride of Yahweh, and the ketubah is the Hebrew Scriptures (our Old Testament), specifically, the Mosaic Covenant (Ex. 19:5) as amplified throughout the Old Testament writings. In the New Testament, the church is identified as the bride of Christ, for which the ketubah is the New Covenant or New Testament, alluded to in the book of Jeremiah chapter 31 verses 31 to 33:

"Behold, days are coming,' declares the LORD, `when I will make a new covenant with the house of Israel and with the house of Judah, not like the covenant which I made with their fathers in the day I took them by the hand to bring them out of the land of Egypt, My covenant which they broke, although I was a husband to them," declares the Lord. "But this is the covenant which I will make with the house of Israel after those days," declares the LORD, "I will put My law within them, and on their heart I will write it; and I will be their God, and they shall be My people."

The author of the epistle to the Hebrews echoes this text for us in Hebrews chapter 8 verses six to thirteen. It states:

"But now hath he obtained a more excellent ministry, by how much also he is the mediator of a better covenant, which was established upon better promises.

For if that first covenant had been faultless, then should no place have been sought for the second.

For finding fault with them, he saith, Behold, the days come, saith the Lord, when I will make a new covenant with the house of Israel and with the house of Judah:

Not according to the covenant that I made with their fathers in the day when I took them by the hand to lead them out of the land of Egypt; because they continued not in my covenant, and I regarded them not, saith the Lord.

For this is the covenant that I will make with the house of Israel after those days, saith the Lord; I will put my laws into their mind, and write them in their hearts: and I will be to them a God, and they shall be to me a people:

And they shall not teach every man his neighbour, and every man his brother, saying, Know the Lord: for all shall know me, from the least to the greatest.

For I will be merciful to their unrighteousness, and their sins and their iniquities will I remember no more.

In that he saith, a new covenant, he hath made the first old. Now that which decayeth and waxeth old is ready to vanish away.

Second Corinthians chapter two verses five and six also states quite clearly: *"And such confidence we have through Christ toward God. Not that we are adequate in ourselves to consider anything as coming from ourselves, but our adequacy is from God, who also made us adequate as servants of a new covenant, not of the letter, but of the Spirit; for the letter kills, but the Spirit gives life."*

The letter is Judgment, justice and punishment or penalty. The law will always make its demands for justice. It continually makes judgment and forever requires punishment. The spirit is grace, mercy and love. When God should have required punishment on us, instead He extended unto us His love; grace and mercy. The letter kills but His spirit gives life eternal.

So it is the word of the Lord Jesus. *"The thief comes but to steal kill and to destroy, but I am come that you might have life and life more abundantly.* We have a marriage contract with God the Father through Christ Jesus. The free gift of God is eternal life. God's love forever interrupts His justice, for He is love!

After the "Ketubah" or contract was agreed to, the agreement was then sealed with the Bride and Groom drinking a poured glass of wine; this was called 'the cup of acceptance'.

The contract we have with God the Father through Jesus Christ His Son and our Lord was ratified by His shed blood. Likewise

He used the wine of the vine symbolic of His shed blood according to Matthew Chapter 26 verse 27-29 which says, *"And he took the cup, and gave thanks, and gave it to them, saying, Drink ye all of it; For this is my blood of the new testament, which is shed for many for the remission of sins."*

So the Lord Jesus having shared the cup of wine with His disciples sealed the New Covenant with them even as in the "Ketubah".

This symbolism is perpetuated in the sacrament of the Holy Communion.

We are commanded by the Lord Jesus to do this. And as often as we do we are to lovingly and longingly remember Him. "Do this in remembrance of me" He said. (Lk.22:19; 1Cor. 11:23-26)

Israel was required to observe the Passover by remembering their deliverance from Egypt's bondage. How God had brought them out by a mighty right hand and destroyed Pharaoh and his host. But here we are told to remember the Lord Jesus Himself who is the Passover Lamb. Remember Him the perfect Lamb of God. He is the lamb slain before the foundations of the world. He gave His life. Shed His blood for our spiritual deliverance—Freeing us from sins bondage, and breaking us from the chains of hell.

I believe then that it is in our best interest to know what is contained in the contract. What are the terms and conditions? As the church of Christ Jesus we need to know what are our entitlements as well as our obligations. Our "Ketubah" contains many glorious promises that we must become acquainted with in order for us to live in earth as the peculiar, holy, royal priesthood of and unto our Lord Most High.

The Lord in the "ketubah" promised He will never leave nor forsake us. He also promised us that what so ever we would ask the Father in His name He shall grant it unto us. (Jn. 15:16)

His name is our Power of Attorney— whatever we ask in His name "Yeshua" in faith believing we shall have. He said "Behold I give you power and authority" Also He said "All power is given unto me both in Heaven and in Earth" in other words I have the power and the authority to assign you this power—It is all legal! "In my name you shall . . ." (Lk.10; Matt. 28)

Every time that I have read the above scripture text, I think of this example: let us imagine for a moment that you are engaged to a powerful man, (or men put yourselves in the place of the powerful man) but this great man must leave you, his fiancée for a while as he returns to his home country to prepare for your coming. Now this well-to-do man loving you his fiancée as much as he does, he puts certain things in place that is necessary to improve and to maintain his Bride's (fiancées) quality of life; satisfactory and well pleasing to him, that speaks to the fine gentle man of excellent means that he is. He sets you up financially. He may say to a local merchant, "anything my fiancée needs

give it to her at my expense." Anything—
do not with hold anything. Nothing is too
good for her. He makes sure that this is well
understood by all. In his absence he wants
you to have the quality of life, the security
that you would as his wife! You can use his
name upon every request.

The marriage is not fully completed but
he assures and he assumes to give to his
bride a quality of life much as she would
have when she is brought to live with him
and they are become husband and wife.
The way I see it, is that it would be to the
Bride groom and his father's shame if the
bride lived below the standard of life they
are able to give to her. The wedding is not
completed but even at this stage she is
considered his bride.

According to ancient customs the Bride
would have also received from her father a
gift which is some what of her inheritance.
Not only that but the Bride price that had
been paid to the father for her, she the bride

is given of that sum. So she is well provided for and her status is much improved.

Although she remained in her parents' house she is not all dependent upon them economically. It is the same for us the church of Jesus the body of Christ whom He has died for. He has made all the necessary arrangements for us to have a specific quality of life while we are here waiting for His return. Therefore when we live below that level, the standard that He has afforded us, we are causing shame and reproach to Him and the Heavenly Father.

He is our source; we are totally in reliance on Him. We trust His love, power, grace and faithfulness. Be not any longer conformed to this world but be ye transformed by the renewing of your minds. That you may prove what is that good and perfect and acceptable will of God. Yes we are living here in earth in Canada, India, Barbados, United States of America, where ever you are but your mind need not be in this three dimensional world that you live in. Set your mind on God. Think God's thoughts, live His way; as He has planned for you, it is Heaven in earth, now!

"Behold, I give you power . . ." It is in the contract, He said it. It is His promise to you 'Bride of Yeshua' do you believe Him? You have to know who you are in relation to Christ Jesus—am I His or not?

And as His, we are to live as His—not in the sweet by and by, not just when He comes to take us home to be with Him, but now! We have the right to the blessing now; I have authority and power this moment, in this time, in this life! As a result of the contract I am exempted from certain calamities.

Your situation is different just because of who you are in Christ Jesus. You shall have plenty even in famine. Remember Isaac. Joseph prospered in Egypt, though he was a foreigner and brought to Egypt as a slave. He was made captain over his captives. When everyone else money failed, Jacob (Israel) had money.

Your situation is different from that of the world.

You will have promotions and raises on your job because you are God's.

For you are a chosen people, a royal priesthood, a holy nation, a people belonging to God, that you may declare the praises of him who called you out of darkness into his wonderful light. (1Pet.2:9)

God will use the issues and circumstances of this world to distinguish us as peculiar unto Him. Others may not be able to get a job in these hard economic times but you shall. Don't assess your outcome base on other people's experiences. It may be so for others not me, am exempted, my situation is different! I will have a favourable outcome. You are peculiar—All to the praise of your great merciful, gracious, faithful and holy God!

You do not have to go through as a hand to mouth, poor wishy washy Christian who must beg and scramble and fight and claw your way through, grudging and begrudging; no you are more than that! You have all the means to be all that God intend for you. He said "If you keep my commands whatsoever you shall ask . . ." if you obey Him as you have contractually agreed to do you will enjoy His bountiful blessings. Our disobedience is what hinders us from fully possessing God's divine will; purpose and blessings for our lives.

Our obedience is of vital necessity. It is still necessary for us to obey God! *"If you fully obey the Lord your God and carefully follow all his commands I give you today, the Lord your God will set you on high above all the nations on earth. All these blessing will come upon you and accompany you if you obey the Lord your God:" (Due.28:1, 2)*

The blessings is not automatic, we must first obey! God is powerful and all wise, but too holy to go back on His word. He says obey!

When we say "Lord" that's what it implies, He is the Head of us, He knows what is best for us—we rely on Him, trusting Him to do what is best for us.

When we through the Holy Spirit was drawn to God in Christ Jesus; being convicted of sin we repented and invited Christ to live and to reign in us; we accepted the terms of the contract, we agreed to the terms of the marriage agreement made. Now live up to your part of the deal which is mainly love, trust and obedience—giving yourself only unto Him.

This is an excerpt from the contract *"If you love me you will keep my command "*(Jn.14:15) we are expected to obey, if we do not obey we do not love Him and therefore are not abiding in Him. It is imperative for us to abide for we cannot bring forth fruit except we abide.

In the Hebrew a fiancée is called a "kudeshet", meaning one who is betrothed, sanctified, dedicated to another. Our part of the agreement is to live as becomes a "Kudeshet", sanctified and dedicated to Him.

So therefore I beseech you brethren that you present your bodies as living sacrifices holy and acceptable unto God which is your reasonable service. (Rom.12:1) It is very fair, seeing He had paid the price for us that we therefore live entirely to and for Him, we are His and not at all our own!

Our posture as we wait for His return should be one of great readiness. As one who is expecting to make their home in another country—we do not fix our focus on where we presently live, as though it be our permanent abode. Regardless of how we love it, all of our heart should be fixed, focused, loving and longing to go to Him, in the home He has prepared for us.

Apostle John talks in the book of Revelation about "loving His appearing." The Bride of Christ will indeed love His appearing. She is anxious to be with her soul's love. The Lord, the Bride Groom is coming back for us, and He is expecting a Bride that is pure radiantly beautiful and having no spots or blemishes. As we wait we must keep our selves pure; Apostle John exhorts us by saying:

"And now, little children, abide in him; that, when he shall appear, we may have confidence, and not be ashamed before him at his coming . . . . We know that, when he shall appear, we shall be like him; for we shall see him as he is. And every man that hath this hope in him purifieth himself, even as he is pure" (1 Jn. 2:28; 3:2-3).

Mohar—The Bride's Price

,

The Bride's Price was a payment from the groom to the bride's father, and was required by the law. Not to be confused with all the other gifts and prices.

A "Mohar" automatically changed the status of the bride; in most cases the Bride price is intended to improve her present personal condition of life, wither she was rich or poor. So though she remained in her parent's house she does so independent of them. She may no longer be a financial responsibility of her parents for the time that she remained with them.

There are many examples of the purchasing of the bride in the Holy Bible, especially the Old Testament: The King desiring Sarah for his wife, of his own initiative offered Abraham a large price for her. He gave him sheep, servants, camels and more. He thought that she was Abraham's sister and available for marriage.

*"And **he entreated Abram well for her sake**: and he had sheep, and oxen, and he asses, and*

menservants, and maidservants, and she asses, and camels." (Gen. 12:16)

Then there was Jacob, he paid for his wife by labor. He worked 7 years in Rachel's father's employ and then to be given another sister in her place—Then he toiled yet another 7 years for Rachel. (Gen.29:20, 27)

Also Isaac's broker acting on Abrahams behalf he paid much for Rebecca, as recorded in Genesis chapter 24.

This could be a very costly venture for the groom I suppose. I would think that he may really want to impress the bride and her parents with his gifts. As this can be easily frown upon as an insult if the price was less than what the parent considered worthy for their daughter. This man and his parents must then be really ready to lavish; go completely over board for her. Giving for her their very best and most valuable possession! There must be a willingness to pay whatever is required and most worthy for the bride. This was the position of

Shechem regarding Dinah the daughter of Jacob and Leah. He desiring her and was willing to go overboard with his gifts.

Genesis 34:12 *Ask me never so much **dowry** and gift, and I will give according as ye shall say unto me: but give me the damsel to wife.*

We have another example in David. This however was the complete opposite. He did not have the financial means to pay for Michal. Silver and gold was not her price. Her father King Saul, sent message to David saying that he does not require any price for the bride but a hundred foreskins of the Philistines. (Saul's intention was to ensnare David.) 1 Samuel 18:25

David however, being the mighty warrior that he was, he fulfilled the ransom for his Bride as is confirmed for us in 2 Samuel chapter 3 and verse 14 when he required his wife of the king.

And David sent messengers to Ishbosheth Saul's son, saying, Deliver me my wife Michal, which

*I **espoused** to me for an hundred foreskins of the Philistines.*

(2 Sam. 3:14)

The book of Ruth is in itself a fascinating love story; of how Boaz as kinsman redeemer (as Jesus is our redeemer) of Naomi and Ruth's inheritance purchased back all their estate. Not only the lands had he bought back but Ruth herself he ransomed for his wife.

"Moreover ***Ruth the Moabitess, the wife of Mahlon, have I purchased to be my wife . . .***" (Ruth 4:10a)

There are very costly prices paid by men for the Brides their hearts were fixated upon, men who would do any thing for the love of their beating hearts.

But there was never such a price required or paid; no never—as that required and paid by our Christ Jesus! Our Father set the highest value for our price, and the Lord Jesus He willingly paid it all in full. The sum He paid was His own life. Unforced, unsolicited; He voluntarily gave the price for His Bride!

"Forasmuch as ye know that ye were not **redeemed** *with corruptible things, as silver and gold . . .*

But **with the precious blood of Christ,** *as of a lamb without blemish and without spot"* 1 Peter 1:18

As it was customary for the father of the Groom to offer a bride-price of great value, indicative of the value He placed on the bride. So it was also that our Heavenly Father offered a price of great value for the bride of His Son. This price was and is to date the greatest price any groom or his father has ever paid for a bride.

He valued us so very highly, the Bible says: *"For God so loved the world that He gave His only begotten son . . ."* (Jn. 3:16)

I said before that the Bride price was a Legal obligation for the Groom and His parents. Even so the Law made its demands on God the Father. He will never violate His own word, but rather He watches over every word to perform it.

"For what the Law could not do, weak as it was through the flesh, God did: sending His own Son in the likeness of sinful flesh and as an offering for sin, He condemned sin in the flesh, in order that the requirement of the Law might be fulfilled in us, who do not walk according to the flesh, but according to the Spirit." (Rom.8:3, 4)

The "mohar" was paid! "You are not your own. For you have been bought with a price . . ." (1 Cor. 6:20) We are also told that our "bride's price" is not that of silver and gold but His precious blood. (I Pet. 1:18-19)

What if the groom could not have paid the price for the bride that he so greatly desired? There must have been occurrences when the groom could not pay the required price.

Suppose Christ could not pay or rather had chosen not to pay the price? Maybe, not even by choice, what if something had prevented Him from going to cross? Understanding that the cross made all the difference, His had to have been the most gruesome death of all ages. It should not be possible for any other creature to die a more horrible death, on the behalf of another person.

It was on the cross that He destroyed the curse from over us. For as it is written "Cursed is any man who hang on a tree." (Gal. 3:13)

It was on the cross that all of our sin was piled upon Him, and He experienced the pain of complete separation from His Father, ever.

God the father turned his back on His beloved Son; it was just then that He looked upon mankind. We were at that moment freed from sin and He was pleased to impute to us His righteousness.

"For he was made sin for us who knew no sin that we might become the righteousness of God in Christ Jesus." God in sending his son in sinful flesh to be a sin offering. By so doing he condemned sin in the flesh. (Rom. 8:3, 4)

It was as a result of our sin. God the Father forsook the Son. He turned His back on His beloved Son, for as it was spoken by the prophet Habakkuk, God cannot look upon sin. The Bible says that it was about the ninth hour Jesus lifted up His voice and cried aloud. "My God my God why have thou forsaken me?" Matt. 27:46. The cross made all the difference!

What if He had died before going to the cross?

Let us look at Him in the moments leading up to His betrayal and arrest in the Garden of Gethsemane. The bible says that there "He agonized". His very sweat became drops of blood.

Medical accounts say, this was the phenomenon of Hematidrosis, or bloody sweat. Being under great emotional stress of the kind our Lord suffered, tiny capillaries in the sweat glands may have broken, thus mixing blood with sweat. And this does not even begin to scratch the surface to the extent of His total suffering, from the garden of Gethsemane to Calvary's crucifixion.

The price He had to pay weighed on Him so heavily. All biblical account further states, that He prayed three sessions of prayer, saying, "Father, if Thou are willing, remove this cup from me: nevertheless not my will, but Thine, be done." (Lk. 22:39-42)

I wonder if maybe the Lord Jesus thought he would have died under the agony— could it have been that He thought that His physical body could not have survived the anguish he endured. And that He would have died there in the garden before He went to the cross; defeating or even aborting His mission.

This sound reasonable, seeing He knew exactly the reason He came into earth was to die the gruesome death of crucifixion. He spoke of it all the time. So for Him at that instant to have asked the Father to use another means does speak to some measure of unwillingness on His part.

I do not believe He was looking for a way of escape, no, but He was securing that His mission was adequately accomplished as planned by the Father.

His Prayer: "Father if thou be willing let this cup pass from me" His Resolve: "Never the less not my will but thine be done."

The scriptures further states "For the joy that was set before Him He endured the cross despised the shame, and is now seated at the right hand of God the Father." (Heb.12:2) Thank God He paid the price in full and purchased us by His Blood!

"And they sang a new song, saying, `Worthy art Thou to take the book, and to break its seals: for Thou wast slain, and didst purchase for God with Thy blood men from every tribe and tongue and people and nation." (Rev. 5:9)

We all realize that our Lord went to the cross for us; we to some degree understand what suffering He endured. But do we fully appreciate how much it cost Him? It cost Him everything, our worth was His life. The Lord Jesus gave His life for His church to purchase her:

Acts 20:28 *"Take heed therefore unto yourselves, and to all the flock, over the which the Holy Ghost hath made you overseers, to feed the church of God, which he hath purchased with his own blood."*

Ephesians chapter 5 verses 25, makes a great comparison and requirement on husbands to love there wives as Christ loves His church. He loves her enough to die for her. He has fulfilled His legal obligation of "The Bride-Price" the "Mohar" is paid and you belong to Him, we are His!

1Cor 6:20 *"For ye are bought with a price: therefore glorify God in your body, and in your spirit, which are God's."*

Mattan—The Voluntary Gift

Bill Risk and others believe that the significance and purpose of the "mattan" was purely social. It was customary for the groom to give presents to his bride at the betrothal; but these gifts were given voluntarily and were never considered to be a legal obligation. There is no biblical legislation found to be connected with this practice.

Although there are a couple of instances recorded where a "mattan" was given or offered in the Bible. Eliezer gave gifts of silver and gold, and garments, to Rebekah. (Gen. 24:) also in Genesis Chapter thirty four, Shechem offered to give anything for Dinah, again this was not the Bride's price but the voluntary gift of the "Mattan", he was willing to grant any request made as a gift to her.

This could be a very extravagant and elaborate act on the part of the prospective groom. Since this was mere custom and not law, the value of the mattan varied significantly and was based solely on the social standing of the groom to be. I would imagine he would want to be as impressive as he possibly can. The Lord Jesus bestows us the wealthiest of gifts. We are given Salvation: His rescuing, saving, preserving. He bestows on us righteousness, grace, peace and joy in the Holy Spirit.

Then there is the "Shiluhim" this is the dowry, the wealth of the bride to be, given her by her father as her share of inheritance.

Remember Rachel and Leah was given Bilha and Zilpa as their slaves, given to them as part of the dowry. Caleb gave his daughter a field and springs of water at Berakah.

The Pharaoh gave his daughter the wife of Solomon the city of Gezer as a wedding gift, and which he called "Shiluhim", "a send-off".

Our Heavenly Father gave us the Comforter. The Holy Spirit, which the Apostle Paul says is our seal of guarantee of our inheritance in Christ Jesus. (Eph. 1:13, 14)

The Lord Jesus our Bride Groom gives us the gift of Eternal life and protection: *"My sheep hear My voice and I know them, and they follow Me; **and I give eternal life to them**, and they shall never perish; and no one shall snatch them out of My hand."* (Jn. 10:27-28)

Again He said, *"Father, the hour has come; glorify Thy Son, that the Son may glorify Thee, even as Thou gavest Him authority over all mankind, that to all who Thou hast given Him, **He may give eternal life."*** (Jn. 17:1-2)

He lavishes us with the gift of **Peace:** *"Peace I leave with you; My peace I give to you; not as the world gives, do I give to you. Let not your heart be troubled, nor let it be fearful."* (John 14:27)

He gives us everything that pertains to life and godliness: *"Again I say to you, that if two of you agree on earth about anything that they may ask, it shall be done for them by My Father who is in heaven. For where two or three have gathered in My name, there I am in their midst."* (Matt. 18:19-20)

In His own words, He said: "And whatever you ask in my name, that will I do, that the Father may be glorified in the Son. If you ask Me anything in My name, I will do it." (Jn.14:14)

Mikveh—The Immersion

The long and very intriguing process of this beautiful and amazing act which originates with our all wise and Eternal Heavenly Father continues. We come to The Mikveh—or Ritual Immersion.

To prepare for betrothal it was the practice that the bride and groom separately do a ritual immersion. This was done prior to entering into the formal betrothal period, and was symbolic of spiritual cleansing. We know that this was also done when Moses consecrated Aaron the High Priest, and his sons the common priests. It was the first item of the requirements in their actual installation service. They had to be washed publicly. It was a public demonstration of an inward purification.

This is one of the church's ordinances that we still practice today, called Baptism. The believers who pledge their life to Christ Jesus is immersed into water. What says the word of the Lord Jesus? "Verily, verily, except a man be born of water and of the

Spirit, he cannot enter into the kingdom of God."

The Lord Jesus did this at the beginning of His earthly ministry. He had to as God required of Aaron and his son, he the Christ, High Priest forever, had to fulfill all righteousness. (Matt.3:13-17; Eph.5:26-27; 1Cor. 6:11). He had to do also as God had prescribed for all who would enter into the Priesthood. It is also a requirement for us. We must do likewise as God has ordained.

According to Joseph Augustus Seiss in his book Holy Types, all men are called to be priest unto God. "God has sent forth and commissioned his ministers to set apart all men to be his priests. And that same commission prescribes how it is to be done; viz. by "baptizing them in the name of the Father, and of the Son, and of the Holy Ghost." Not merely by the outward application of water to them in solemn religious service; but also "teaching them to observe all things whatsoever Jesus has commanded." Our washing is not a mere external rite, but an inward grace, "the answer of a good conscience toward God." It is not mere water; but water joined with the word of God, in which we by faith receive the cleansing and renewing efficacy of the Holy Ghost. A man may be outwardly baptized, and still be impure," but he cannot spiritually apprehend, appropriate, and enter into his baptism, without becoming a renewed and sanctified man. Nay, his whole spiritual renovation is included in this washing; so that his baptism is virtually no baptism at all, unless attended or followed by the death and burial of the old man of sin, and the planting in the soul of a new, pure and vigorous righteousness."

(The Gospel in Leviticus, page 145, paragraphs 1 and two)

After the couple had completed the Mikveh or their spiritual cleansing, they would appear together under a Huppah—the wedding canopy. The wedding canopy served to symbolize a new household in the making. (Ps. 19:5; Joel 2:16).

So standing under the canopy they would publicly express their intention of becoming betrothed. It was also that during this time they would do the exchanging of gifts. This was followed by the two sharing a cup of wine to seal their betrothal vows.

At the conclusion of this particular ceremony the couple was regarded to have entered into the betrothal agreement. They were considered by this time married, but the marriage was not to be consummated, no sexual relations were to have happened as yet.

So the couple remained apart, living separately until the end of the betrothal, which was typically expected to be for a period of one year.

We see this time of betrothal illustrated in the gospels accounts of the marital status of Joseph and Mary. (Mat. 1:18-25).

Also when God had brought Israel through the red sea and He told Moses to have them gathered at the base of the mountain, Sinai. The Bible said that the glory of the Lord covered the mountain. When His glory covered the tabernacle it was a type of the Huppah (wedding canopy) the two, God and Israel entered into their betrothal. God said to Israel, "If you will obey and keep . . ." (Ex 19:5). They responded, "All we will do!" (Ex 19:8) they accepted the proposal. But we know that Israel broke her wedding vows and as required by the Torah or law she was put out, she went into exile. (Due 24:1, 2) "I will judge you as a woman who has broken wedlock." (Ez.14:28)

However God has a plan for Israel's restoration. "You play the harlot," said God, "but return unto Me."

But how is their return base on the requirement of the law possible? It is only possible through death. Their return is only possible by the death of a spouse, one of them must die. And it is for that reason

God incarnate died. By His death the first contract that had been broken is made void. Now are they able to return again in marriage covenant to another; (Christ Jesus) though He be the same Husband (God the Father).

The spouse dies annulling or cancelling the old contract, and then He is resurrected to life again. She the bride (Israel) must also die to the flesh and be born again. "You must be born again" said the Lord Yeshua to Nichodemus the Jewish ruler. (Jn.3:1-21)

Apostle Paul knew the law and ancient Hebrew customs. This is how he addressed this matter of the law. He said, "... *the law has authority over a man only as long as he lives. For example, by the law a married woman is bound to her husband as long as he is alive, but if her husband dies, she is released from the of marriage. So then, if she marries another man while her husband is still alive, she is called an adulteress. But if her husband dies she is released from that law and is not an adulteress even though she marries another. **Even so my brothers, you***

also died to the law through the body of Christ that you might belong to another, *to him who was raised from the dead, in order that we bear fruit to God."* (Rom 7:1-4.)

Many are of the opinion that God has completely cut off His people. But the scripture do not teach anything of the sort. There is a planned return for God's chosen people. And that way is Christ Jesus. He wants them back—"Come now, let us reason together," says the LORD. "Though your sins are like scarlet, they shall be as white as snow; though they are red as crimson, they shall be like wool."(Is.1:18)

God is by nature love; He is love. This means that He will always demonstrate grace and mercy to and for His people.

His attributes is Elohim or God is justice strict judgment and lawgiver. Yahweh represents His attributes mercy, love and forgiveness. If God will deal with his people by strict judgment or justice we would not have a chance! But He deals with us with balance of 1 part of justice to 2 parts mercy.

"Yahweh, Yahweh Elohim!" (Ex.34: 6) God describes himself as two times merciful and once strict judge."

YAHWEH in the Scriptures (Gen. 2:4, "These are the generations of the heavens and of the earth when they were created, in the day that **YAHWEH Elohim** made the earth and the heavens.")—"~yhil{a/ hw"hy>—*HaSHEM God*. This is the first mention in the Torah of the Hebrew four-letter Name **h-w-h-y, YAHWEH which denotes God in His Attribute of Mercy**. At first, God created the world exclusively with the Attribute of Justice [*Elohim*], because the ideal state is for Man to be judged according to his deeds, without a need for special mercy, but God knew that Man cannot survive without mercy and forbearance. Therefore **He added the Name signifying mercy**, to teach that He would temper justice with compassion (*Rashi* to 1:1). The Name **h-w-h-y** also signifies the eternity of God, because its letters are also those of the words hy<h>wI hw<ho hy"h",

He was, Is, and will be . . . ." (*The Stone Edition of The Chum ash*, p. 11)

The Rabbis Spake about the same commentary on the Sacred Name in Ex. 3:13-15 when the Name was given to Moses because he asked Him what His name was—*What is His Name?* Obviously the Jews knew the various names of God, so that the question cannot be understood literally. God has many Names, each of which represents the way in which He reveals Himself through His behavior toward the world. **When He is merciful, He is called** *HaSHEM* **[h-w-h-y], the Name that represents compassion**. This Name also represents the eternity of God, for it is composed of the letters that spell hy<h>wI hw<ho hy"h", *He was, He is, and He will be*, meaning that God's Being is timeless. When He exercises strict judgment, He is called *Elohim*. When He exercises His mastery over nature and performs hidden miracles—as He did for the Patriarchs—He is called *Shaddai*, and so on. Thus Moses was saying that once the Jews accepted

him as God's emissary, they would want to know which of God's attributes He would manifest in the course of redeeming them from Egypt (*Rambam*)

Kiddushim—The Sanctification

According to the Jewish scholars this period of the betrothal, called kiddushim means "sanctification" or "set apart." This word really defines the purpose of the betrothal period. It was a time in which the couples were to set themselves apart and to prepare to enter into the covenant of marriage.

The Jewish understanding of betrothal has always been much stronger than our modern western engagement. It really does not equal in any way.

The betrothal was so binding that the couple would need a religious divorce in order to annul the contract (Deut. 24:1-4). This was an option available only to the Groom, as the Bride had no say in any divorce proceedings. And it was not a simple matter for the man to get a divorce either. She, the bride had to have thoroughly misrepresented herself to the groom and or have conducted herself rather immorally; completely unacceptable according to the commands of God.

During this time of Betrothal the groom returned to his father's house and the bride awaited his return for her.

The custom was for the bride groom to return to his father's house to prepare the matrimonial home, to bring his wife into and unto him. However it was the responsibility of his father to determine when the house was adequately suited and ready for the bride. Not until the Father said "go get your bride" can He bring her to his home.

No one but the father fixed the time for the grooms return. The Grooms job was to build the room, fix it as best as he possibly could and when it was to standard, up to par, proper to the father, then and only then the father gave his approval.

The Groom of course had some knowledge of the approximate time. He was working with this time in mind and of course he did not want any delays. So he gave it his best; looking longingly to that day when his work is done, the room is completed and the long hard separation comes to an end. But only the father knew the precise time that his son should go for his bride.

Similarly it is that no one knows the time or the hour that the Bride Groom shall return.

In Token and in Pledge the Lord Jesus said in John chapter 14 and verses 1 to 3: *"I go to prepare a place for you that where I am there you may be also."*

This is in covenant and was actually a part of the vows spoken by the groom to his bride. Just as He had promised He will do. His words will not pass away! He is there preparing for us to join Him, but the thing is, no one but the Father knows what time His returning will be.

So He comes to his bride as a thief in the night. It was the practice that the groom would come at night.

He, the groom does not send messengers a week or two prior to his arrival to say I will be coming to you on such and such a day.

She should be ready; her family, the bridal party and all the invitees are expecting him to come to take her at any given time. She should be already making and keeping herself beautiful. Her gown all made and ready for the final ceremony. And all necessary arrangements finalized. She was to be packed, and anxiously awaiting her groom's return.

So it is for the Church. The Lord instructs us to watch and pray, to look up and be ready. He said "as it was in the day of Noah."

"But as the days of Noah were, so shall also the coming of the Son of man be. For as in the days that were before the flood they were eating and drinking, marrying and giving in marriage, until the day that Noe entered into the ark, and knew not until the flood came, and took them all away; so shall also the coming of the Son of man be."
(Mat. 24:37-39)

So what was it like in the days of Noah, before he entered into the ark? Genesis chapter six, verses five, eleven and twelve informs us: ". . . *And God saw that the wickedness of man was great in the earth, and that every imagination of the thoughts of his heart was only evil continually. The earth also was corrupt before God, and the earth was filled with violence. And God looked upon the earth, and, behold, it was corrupt; for all flesh had corrupted his way upon the earth . . ."*

So the earth in the days of Noah was full of people who did not know God, who lived after the lust of their own flesh, in evil, corrupt and violent ways. They did not believe that God was going to send a great flood. They mocked the prophet of God! And everyone did as it pleased him. The bible says, "God saw this great wickedness, *and it repented the LORD that he had made man on the earth, and it grieved him at his heart."* (Gen.6:6)

We cannot imagine the anguish of our loving Heavenly Father when He looked down upon the earth and saw no one (except Noah) living a godly life. It was so bad that God brought an end to all flesh of that day except for Noah's eight. *"The end of all flesh is come before me."* God will only bear with people's wicked ways for so long, before Judgment comes upon them— He will not always chide with man!

It was life as usual and then it happened as though suddenly. He said His coming will be as a thief in the night, there is no warning given. He comes in a moment when we think not. So there must be watchfulness on our part.

Luke Chapter twelve and verses thirty five to forty instructs: *"Be dressed ready for service and keep your lamps burning, [36] like servants waiting for their master to return from a wedding banquet, so that when he comes and knocks they can immediately open the door for him. [37] It will be good for those servants whose master finds them watching when he comes. Truly I tell you, he will dress himself to serve, will have them recline at the table and will come and wait on them. [38] It will be good for those servants whose master finds them ready, even if he comes in the middle of the night or toward daybreak. [39] But understand this: If the owner of the house had known at what hour the thief was coming, he would not have let his house be broken into. 40 You also must be ready, because the Son of Man will come at an hour when you do not expect him."*

For the ready bride His coming should not be sudden or unexpected. It should not take her unaware as the coming of a thief. Because she is expecting him, she is waiting for him; the light is on, and she is watching and praying. She anxiously waits for his appearing!

We must in like manner wait for the Lord Jesus. Expect Him and in such expectancy make ourselves ready for Him.

In the Gospel of Mathew chapter twenty five and verses one to thirteen the Lord Jesus gives the parable of the ten virgins. They are divided into two distinctive groups, one wise and the other foolish. The Bible says that these ten virgins all took oil in their lamps, but the difference between them was that the wise took extra oil; they were prepared for the unexpected. In the event that the bridegroom may be delayed, they would need more oil.

The foolish however had no such consideration. Then it happened, in the still quiet watch of the late night, came the cry; "behold the bridegroom cometh go ye out to meet Him!" You can well imagine the chaos, the panic of the foolish as they were awakened and found themselves in darkness or their lamps dimmed. The lights of their lamps going out! Lend me some oil were their cry to the wise, just a little bit— just enough to get me out the door. But all their desperate efforts will be entirely for nought, it was too late!

The wise virgins had made themselves adequately ready—not just waiting but ready!

Have you ever had to pick up, or give an individual a ride to somewhere? And on your way you purposed to phone the person, making sure that they are on time. You informed them that you are 5 minutes away, come outside, or come down stairs, what ever the case maybe. Their reply to you—"okay I am ready" but you got there and they were nowhere in sight, and you were made to wait.

So many people confuse getting ready, with being ready. You are not ready when you are styling your hair; you are still not ready if you can't find one foot of the shoes you need to wear. If you are looking for the house keys or for the keys to the car and are unable to find them—you are still not ready. If you are in the process of changing your clothes for what so ever reason, you are not ready!

You are only ready when everything that is necessary for the occasion is in place, personal and other wise. There is nothing else for you to do than to wait; that is what readiness is!

Is your garment spotless, are they whiter than snow?

You are ready if your attire is in place; it is brilliant white, having no spot or wrinkles. Revelation 19:8 says, the white garment is the righteous acts of the Saints. The righteous deeds done is the white robe of the bride, how white is your robe, is it even white at all?

We cannot be contented to say we are ready and our children, wife, husband, parent, friend and neighbors are still outside of the Kingdom of God. There is an urgency. We must get about this thing of preaching the gospel to every ethnicity, baptizing them in the name of the Father and the Son and the Holy Spirit! It is each of our responsibility to make other disciples.

Nissuin—The Carry Away of the Bride

We have come to the final stage in the wedding process—the "Nissuin" which means, "To carry." This is very descriptive as it was literally the event culminating the Marriage. The Groom took his bride and carried her off to her new home in his father's house.

So the Father as was the traditional thing for Him to do has given His approval for the wedding ceremony to begin, and the Groom is on his way to his Bride. She is, or should be ready and waiting for the sound—the shout.

Customarily the groom's man or groom's party goes ahead of the bridegroom, leading the way to the bride's house and he would shout *"Behold, the bridegroom comes."*

This would be followed by the sounding of the trumpet. At the sounding of the trumpet the entire wedding party would be gathered. And the wedding procession would go through the streets of the city to the marriage ceremony. The groomsmen once again set up the Huppah and the couple would say a blessing over a cup of wine. The wine would be blessed with the ritual prayer: "Blessed art Thou, Eternal our God, Creator of Heaven and Earth, who has given us the fruit of the vine . . ." This ceremony finalized the promises and vows.

The high point of the festive celebration was the wedding Supper. This was not at all like our typical western wedding reception.

These festivities were actually seven days of merriment. Afterwards the groom was free to bring his bride to their new home, the room he had prepared for them to live together as husband and wife in the full covenant of marriage.

The words of the wedding ceremony are from Psalm 45 and Isaiah 61:10-62:5 – ". . . *as the bridegroom rejoices over the bride, so shall Elohim rejoice over you.*" Once the ceremony is over, the two go into the bridal chamber for 7 days. These seven days period represent to me the time of the seven years of tribulation. The beginning of which is the very moment the church is carried away to be with the Bridegroom.

The Songs of Solomon, read during Passover, gives us the details of the intimacy between the Lord Jesus and His Bride.

Yedidah writes in his writings "Ancient Jewish wedding" saying:

"The seven days in the chamber correspond to the seven days between the end of the Feast of Trumpets, and the Day of Atonement, when the High Priest takes the blood before the altar of Yahuweh, and the sins of the nation of Israel are forgiven." He further states that, "At the end of the 7 days, the groom's "friend" (or Elijah—John the baptiser came in the spirit of Elijah, and represented Messiah, and called himself the "friend of the Bridegroom" in John 3:29), or "witness", waits at the chamber door. The guests have arrived and are waiting for the door to be opened, and the wedding banquet to begin. When the groom is ready, he knocks from the inside of the door of the chamber, indicating that they are ready to make their public appearance before everyone. The friend opens the door, and the guests cheer.

In Revelation 11, the two witnesses have been in the earth witnessing and preparing for 3 ½ years. At the voice of the Bridegroom calling them up, Messiah Yahushua comes out of heaven with a trumpet blast, accompanied by the set-apart ones who have died, to gather His whole Bride for the wedding, and the 7 days in the chuppah. The door of heaven opens and He proceeds out. The "bride has made herself ready". He picks up His Bride who is alive and waiting for Him on the earth. Then after His glorious entrance into Jerusalem, they proceed to the wedding feast. Some believe that the wedding feast will occur at Mt. Sinai, since that is where the terms of the marriage Covenant were given to the Bride. Look at the wording of Revelation 19:8 and 11. The parable of the wise virgins, of Matthew 25:1-11, shows us that only the prepared Bride gets to go into the chuppah with Him. The guests are shut out."

Let us again compare the "Carry away" to the coming of our Lord Jesus to take away His bride with Him. Similarly He does not know the time or the hour, as He told the disciples in Matthew chapter twenty four and verses thirty two to thirty six. Of course He is all knowing. There is nothing hid from Him, but He must wait for the Father's consent, approval and command— "Go get your bride!" He does nothing of himself. He does only the will of the Father!

Another similarity between the ancient Jewish wedding customs and that of Christ and the church is that there shall be a shout "behold the Bride Groom Cometh!" the bible says that the Trumpet of God shall be sounded. This shout will announce His return. It is the sound that we are anxiously waiting for. This is a very distinctive and glorious sound.

Even the dead in Christ would be awakened by the sound. It is powerful. The dead in Christ from everywhere, without regard for depth, height or weight all shall be awakened and gathered by this great sound!

Apostle Paul in his letter to the Thessalonians says. *"For the Lord himself will come down from heaven, with a loud command, with the voice of the archangel and with the trumpet call of God, and the dead in Christ will rise first. After that, we who are still alive and are left will be caught up together with them in the clouds to meet the Lord in the air. And so we will be with the Lord forever.* (1Thess. 4:16)

We shall all be gathered together in the heavenly procession. He will carry us away to the Marriage Supper of the Lamb and to our home; the mansions which He promised to prepare for us and there shall we be with the Lord for evermore.

"Let us rejoice" says John, "and be glad and give him glory! For the wedding of the Lamb has come, and his bride has made herself ready. Fine linen, bright and clean, was given her to wear. (Fine linen stands for the righteous acts of God's holy people.)Then the angel said to me, "Write this: Blessed are those who are invited to the wedding supper of the Lamb!" And he added, "These are the true words of God." (Rev 19:7-9).

Blessed are they who are invited. I say also, blessed are they who would accept the invitation. It is one thing for the host to send the invitations to the intended guests, but what if the invitations are not acknowledged? The earnest is on the invitees to accept the request. Many have completely rejected the invitation. We hear there excuses all the time. But I pray that this book will awake the consciousness of someone to their commitment to God.

That you will not be one of those to hear the Lord Say, "Too late!"

There is the parable that the Lord Jesus told in the Gospel. He said: "A certain man was preparing a great banquet and invited many guests. At the time of the banquet he sent his servant to tell those who had been invited, 'Come, for everything is now ready.'

"But they all alike began to make excuses. The first said, 'I have just bought a field, and I must go and see it. Please excuse me.'

"Another said, 'I have just bought five yoke of oxen, and I'm on my way to try them out. Please excuse me.'

"Still another said, 'I just got married, so I can't come.'

"The servant came back and reported this to his master. Then the owner of the house became angry and ordered his servant, 'Go out quickly into the streets and alleys of the town and bring in the poor, the crippled, the blind and the lame.' 'Sir,' the servant said, 'what you ordered has been done, but there is still room.'

"Then the master told his servant, 'Go out to the roads and country lanes and compel them to come in, so that my house will be full. I tell you, not one of those who were

invited will get a taste of my banquet.'"
Luke 14:17-23

The invitation is still open. Please do accept.
Let your response be—"Yes, attending!"

Part 2

The Rehearsals

The Holy Bible is filled with much of what are referred to as Shadows and Types. God had chosen Israel for the purpose of demonstrating His love for all of humanity. He willing and lovingly reveals to us His very intentions, His heart.

I never understood clearly what the word "Rehearsal" really meant for this book. I have pondered it for months since I received the vision. Let me explain, that this book is in direct response to a vision I had. I saw something like a book cover or card, almost exactly as this book cover is and bearing the titles exactly as it appears. So this book from cover to cover is a vision. There were no lightning flashing, no thunder rolling; no great noises, not even the direct voice of God. I was on an Island though, but not pathmos.

From the moment I saw the vision I pondered and questioned its meaning. I thought that I would make sense of it all before I try to write. Honestly it did not happen that way. I couldn't understand the significance of

"Rehearsal" paired with "Preparing for the Bridegroom" not until this moment, it is all so very clear, now as am about to attempt writing this segment on the "Rehearsal".

It is indeed as though the scales have fallen from my eyes. There are no clouds in view and I peer as though directly into God's scopes and I get it, I understand it!

What I said before of "the ancient Jewish marriage customs". All these are shadows and types of the Old Testament. The Holy Days and or Feast Days; all the customs and practices, are leading to the time when all things will be as the heavenly Father intends, planned and purposed for us.

Veiled in all of these types and shadows we find a decadent foretaste of what is to come. Now we see in part and we understand in part. But when that which is perfect shall come, then all that is in part shall be done away with. (1Cor.13:10) The shadow is met by the reality—Yeshua our Christ. *"These are shadow of the things that were to come; the reality, however, is found in Christ.* (Col.2:17)

Let us try to understand the meaning of "Rehearsal" We must first understand that the Jews or Hebrew people are observers of specific religious ceremonies called "Holy Days" or "Feast Days". These are required observances ordained and commanded by God.

The word "festival" or "feast," in Hebrew is *hag* or *mo'ed*, meaning a "set time" or "appointed time." An appointed "festival" or "feast" is a "holy convocation" or "Sacred Assembly".

The term "sacred assembly" in Hebrew is *mikrah*, a "Rehearsal" or "recital." So the meaning of "Rehearsal" is "sacred assembly" the means by which God the Father has chosen to reveal His great love for humanity through His Son messiah Yeshua.

Therefore, for Jews and non-Jews alike, all of the festivals and feasts appointed by God as "Rehearsals" are for the purpose of revealing the Messiah (Col. 2:16, 17) and completing God's overall Plan of salvation for Humanity.

Think for a moment of a wedding or dress rehearsal, what it is, but an attempt to perfect the actual wedding day or event; the ceremony, dress, dinner party and even entertainment. Everything is choreographed to happen in precision and exactness, flawlessly! It is not the actual event but it is a very good indication, and representation of what is to be expected. We see now in a glass darkly, don't we?

When we shall join the Lord Jesus at the Wedding Supper of the Lamb and we shall then live and reign with Him—there shall we and all that we do be perfect, and complete. We will understand it better!

I think one of the gravest errors of the Christian church is to have strayed so far from the holy days which the Lord had ordained and set forth through His chosen people Israel in the Holy Bible. A better understanding of the holy days does open for us a greater comprehension of the scriptures, and enable us to better interpret the times and there relations to the Lord Jesus and His church.

I will attempt a couple of examples to help us to better understand what Holy Spirit is intending. What He is revealing unto us the church of Yeshua. I must however first admit that I do not have a very thorough or absolute understanding of the Holy days and all of there relevance to the church today. All that I am doing is to speak to you on the basis that the Lord by Holy Spirit is presently speaking to me. What I am setting forth is by revelation knowledge, coupled with my personal researches on various topics significant to the general contents of this book.

I know that God has a plan for us. I believe that God reveals His plan through the Holy Days or Feast days that He inaugurated with Israel and are written in the Holy Scriptures.

The Holy Days, or Feast Days, fall during three seasons of the year. They are the early spring harvest, late spring harvest and early autumn harvest. These days give a portrayal of God's spiritual harvest of humankind to eternal life.

This was what the Lord Jesus Christ spoke of, when the Samaritan woman believed and was saved; she and her city went into a two days revival with Yeshua [Jesus]. He said to the disciples—"There is that saying that there is still four months to the harvest; but lift up your eyes and see the fields are already white and ready to be harvested." (Jn. 4: 35-38)

These observances serve as timeless reminders for us, revealing God's divine plan of Salvation for all of humanity. They reveal the unfolding of God's plan for mankind and how He will establish His Kingdom on earth.

This is the good news, or gospel, Jesus Christ preached after John was put in prison and subsequently beheaded. The Bible says that He went into Galilee, proclaiming the good news of God. "The time has come," he said. "The kingdom of God has come near.

Repent and believe the good news!" (Mk. 1:14-15). In other words the "Good News" is that the "Kingdom of God is come".

This is God's great plan. The apostle Paul refers it as a mystery, or secret. "By His wisdom He planned before "the foundation of the world." (Eph.1:4) "He has made known to us his secret purpose, in accordance with the plan which he determined beforehand in Christ, to be put into effect when the time was ripe: namely, that the universe, everything in heaven and earth, might be brought into unity in Christ. In Christ indeed we have been given our share in this heritage, as was decreed in his design whose purpose is everywhere at work" (Eph. 1:9-11, Revised English Bible).

The Holy Days, Feast Days or the "Rehearsal" help us to see the great master plan—the very purpose of God and how we truly become His people.

Notice this description of our destiny: *"Behold, the tabernacle of God is with men, and He will dwell with them, and they shall be His people."* Revelation chapter 21 and verse three says "God Himself will be with them and be their God." Step by step, the Holy Days reveal for us how this Glorious portrait will become a reality.

Leviticus Chapter twenty three presents to us a list of the Holy Days: The Passover, Feast of Unleavened Bread, the Feast of Firstfruit, Feast of Pentecost, the Feast of Tabernacles, The Festival of Trumpets, and the Day of Atonement. When God gave these seven Holy Days to Moses, He instructed him to make it clear that these were His appointed feast, that they are His Festivals. They are sacred assemblies or "Rehearsals"! (Lev. 23:1-4)

"The LORD said to Moses, "Speak to the Israelites and say to them: 'These are my appointed festivals, the appointed festivals of the LORD, which you are to proclaim as sacred assemblies."

In Zachariah Chapter fourteen and verse sixteen the sentence is passed on all who will not observe the "Feast of Tabernacles".

"If any of the peoples of the earth do not go up to Jerusalem to worship the King, the LORD Almighty, they will have no rain. If the Egyptian people do not go up and take part, they will have no rain.

The LORD will bring on them the plague he inflicts on the nations that do not go up to celebrate the Festival of Tabernacles. This will be the punishment of Egypt and the punishment of all the nations that do not go up to celebrate the Festival of Tabernacles."

Let us take a look and see the fascinating purpose of each of God's Holy Days, along with their promises of hope for mankind."

The Lord Jesus and the Apostle along with the believers of the early Church observed these Holy Feasts.

The Expositor's Bible Commentary, in a reference to Acts 20:6, notes that Paul, unable to arrive at Jerusalem for the Passover, "remained at Philippi to celebrate it and the week-long Feast of Unleavened Bread . . ." (Richard N. Longenecker, Zondervan,

Grand Rapids, 1981, Vol. 9, p. 507). Regarding Acts 20:16, the same commentary notes that Paul "wanted, if at all possible, to get to Jerusalem for Pentecost on the fiftieth day after Passover . . ." (p. 510).

The Apostle Paul's ministry included observing the Holy Days with the Church. In defending the gospel he preached, Paul said he brought the same message the other apostles taught: "Therefore, whether it was I or they, so we preach and so you believed"
(1 Cor.15:11).

Paul and all the apostles taught a consistent message of the Christian's obligation to follow the example of Jesus Christ in all matters. The Apostle John summed up this message: "He who says he abides in Him ought himself also to walk just as He walked"
(1 Jn. 2:6).

Jewish believers continued to uphold the Holy Days, as did gentile Christians. Col. 2:16 Shows Gentile Christians Kept the Holy Days. From all these references we can conclude only that the practice of the early

Church was to continue the observance of these God-given festivals.

As I have said before; the "Rehearsal" are namely, the Spring Feast and the Fall Feast. The first of these "Rehearsal" are the four "Spring Feast" they are: "Passover", then the "Feast of Unleavened Bread", "Feast of First Fruit", followed by the "Festival of Pentecost".

The Final of the "Rehearsals" are the last three feast, referred to as the "Fall Festivals" they are namely, "Feast of Trumpets", "Feast of Atonement" and "Feast of Tabernacles". These Fall Feast or latter rain feast, are yet to be fulfilled. Their fullness or substance is in Christ Yeshua alone.

The Passover

Every Christian believer obviously knows and is very well acquainted with the death or crucifixion of Jesus Christ, for the purpose of forgiving our sins. But do we really understand the significance and the necessity of His very cruel death on the cross. Let us take a look at just how the death of the Lord Jesus Christ is reflected in God's Holy Feast Days or "Rehearsal".

First—the Sacrifice of Jesus Christ the Son of God is the central event in the plan of God for the salvation of humankind.

The Lord Jesus speaking of His eminent death, He said, *"The son of man must be lifted up, even as Moses lifted up the serpent in the wilderness, so that whoever believes in Him should not perish but have eternal life. For God so loved the world that He gave His only begotten Son, that whoever believes in Him should not perish but have everlasting life"* (Jn. 3:14-16).

His sacrifice, the central message of the Passover, was a supreme act of love for humankind. This important event laid the foundation for the remaining annual

Holy Days and Festivals. It is the most momentous step in God's plan. The Lord Jesus also said:

"For this purpose I came to this hour . . . And I, if I am lifted up from the earth, will draw all peoples to Myself" (Jn. 12:27, 32).

The day on which this profound event, the crucifixion, transpired was the 14th day of the first month of God's calendar, the same day on which the Passover lambs were to be killed (Lev. 23:5). (God's Holy Day Plan, The Promise of Hope for All Mankind—ucg.org)

The point made is that Jesus was the sacrificial lamb for that year's Passover.

Paul later wrote the congregation at Corinth that, *"Christ, our Passover, was sacrificed for us" (1 Cor. 5:7).* Not only was He the sacrifice for that year but for all time, He is our Passover!

Now let us look back through the Holy Scriptures the Bible for the instructions and meaning God gave concerning this particular day. I hope we will in our efforts find a greater understanding of what God the Father intended and what He expects from us as far as observing this Feast Day— "Passover" is concern.

God's Passover instructions to Moses were as follows: He said, tell Pharaoh *"let My people go, that they may hold a "feast" to Me in the wilderness"* (Ex. 5:1). He unleashed a series of plagues upon Egypt and all the time hardening the heart of Pharaoh. Then by a great and mighty hand delivered Israel out of Egypt's clinch; freeing them from their enslavement in Egypt. There were a total of 10 plagues which struck the oppressors of God's people. But His instructions regarding the 10th plague, and Israel's obligation for their escape only came to them after the 9th plague which struck the tyrant Egypt.

God gave Moses very specific commands Concerning His plans and intentions for His people on the night of the first Passover. These instructions were the means by which the Israelites were to be securely sheltered and saved. The death angel would on the dead of night pass through Egypt, killing the first born of every house which had not the particular symbol representing God's plan of salvation. The blood of the sacrificial lamb or goat was to be painted on the door post of their houses.

These were the specific commands God spoke to Moses, He said: "On the 10th day of the first month, each Israelite was to select a lamb or goat large enough to feed each household" (Ex. 12:3). The animal to be slain was to be a yearling male, without any sort of defect. On the 14th day of that month at evening, the Israelites were to kill the animals and place some of the blood on the doorposts of their homes. The animals were then to be roasted and eaten along with unleavened bread and bitter herbs.

The Israelites, on this night, the actual night of the "Passover" hurriedly ate this meal as they escaped Egypt.

The Lord further instructed, that on the same evening He would kill all the firstborn of Egypt to convince Pharaoh to release the Israelites from slavery.

The firstborn of each Israelite family would be protected if the sign of His "salvation" the blood of the slain lamb were present on the entrances to their homes. The death angel would pass over as long as there where the evidence of the death of the required sacrifice on the entrance to the home. No death will come upon the Israelites household.

The life of the first born of the house bearing the blood of the unspotted, unblemished year old lamb or goat slain would be spared. He said, *"When I see the blood I will pass over you."* Any house not bearing the blood of the required sacrifice, their first born would be killed. So here is the obvious meaning to the observance of "Passover" (Vs. 13).

God said that this day was to be unto Israel a memorial forever. *"And you shall keep it as a feast to the LORD throughout your generations.*

"You shall keep it as a feast by an everlasting ordinance" (vs. 14).

In Leviticus chapter twenty three and verse four the Lord made it clear that the "Passover Feast" was His and it was to be a Holy convocation "Rehearsal" unto Him.

The Passover is symbolic of Jesus Christ the perfect Lamb of God; the "Passover Lamb" slain before the foundations of the world. All of the sacrifices offered until the time of Jesus Christ was done in faith, pointing to His death, for the atonement of the sins of the world. Abel, Noah, Job, Abraham, Isaac and Jacob all sacrificed in faith believing in what they had not seen.

Though they had not laid eyes on Him, they looked by faith. Even as Job declared: "For I know that my redeemer lives and I shall see Him for myself and not another! (Job 19: 27)

The Passover observance was to symbolize The Lord Jesus Christ's death. In 1Corinthians chapter 5 and verse 7 the

Apostle Paul referred to the Lord Jesus Christ as "our Passover" Also John the Baptizer identified Him; pointing Him out to the crowd. They wanted to know if John was the messiah they were anticipating. But he pointing in the direction of the approaching Jesus, exclaimed: *"behold the Lamb of God who takes away the sin of the world!"*(Jn.1:29)

Like John I call your attention, look! Look at God's "Passover Lamb"!

Our Lord Jesus was that unblemished male. He was the perfect sacrifice, not having any spot or blemish. He had no imperfections; completely sinless, but He became sin for us. He who knew no sin, the righteous and holy took our sin and penalty upon Himself. By His shed blood we are forgiven and made free.

So it is, "Therefore, just as sin entered the world through one man, and death through sin, and in this way death came to all people, because all sinned—(Rom. 5:12) "For the wages of sin is death, but the gift of

God is eternal life in Christ Jesus our Lord."
(Rom. 6:23). "So is the gift not like it was by
one that sinned: for the judgment was by
one to condemnation, but the free gift is of
many offenses unto justification."

*"Then Christ would have had to suffer many
times since the creation of the world. But now
he has appeared once for all at the end of the
ages to do away with sin by the sacrifice of
himself."(Heb.9:26)*

Because He lives we live also. I make
emphasis here, the Lord Jesus—He
redeemed us, atoned our sins. We are
forgiven, pardoned, sins forgotten,
consciences purged of guilt.

As far as the east is from the west, so far
has He removed our transgression from us.
(Ps. 103:12) The price has been paid in full.
So we the guilty walk away free, because
the sinless Christ paid the price by offering
Himself, "the Lamb of God which takes
away the sins of the world!"

"Christ came as High Priest of the good things to come . . . not with the blood of goats and calves, but with His own blood He entered the Most Holy Place once for all, having obtained eternal redemption." (Heb.9:11-12)

The Lord Yeshua our Christ bought us with His precious blood! On the last night with the disciples at what we call the last supper. He instituted new Passover symbols and practices to teach important truths about Himself and God's continuing plan of salvation.

The apostle John describes for us the events of the Lord Jesus' last evening with His disciples:

"Now before the feast of the Passover, when Jesus knew that His hour had come that He should depart from this world to the Father, having loved His own who were in the world, He loved them to the end." During the meal Jesus *"rose from supper and laid aside His garments, took a towel and girded Himself. After that, He poured water into a basin and began to wash the disciples' feet, and to wipe*

them with the towel with which He was girded"
(Jn.13:1-5)

In the Gospel according to Matthew, chapter twenty six and verses twenty-six to thirty gives an account of their Passover meal that night before He was betrayed. The verses say that "While they were eating, Jesus took bread, gave thanks and broke it, and gave it to his disciples, saying, "Take and eat; this is my body."

The particular meal for the evening supper would have included flat, or unleavened bread. In fact three cakes of unleavened bread were on the table in front of the host. The Lord Yeshua took the **center** one and broke it into little pieces. The three cakes were said to represent the Trinity, with the center cake representing the Son or Messiah. When He took this bread (probably the center cake) and broke it, He said, *"This is My body."*

This bread was broken into little pieces to remind them that a slave never had a whole loaf, but only fragments to eat" (Barclay, p. 22).

This is exactly who the messiah became for us. A bond servant, or slave according to Philippians chapter 2 verses 6-8:

"Who, being in the form of God, thought it not robbery to be equal with God: But made himself of no reputation, and took upon him the form of a servant, and was made in the likeness of men: And being found in fashion as a man, he humbled himself, and became obedient unto death, even the death of the cross."

The Bible says "Then he took the cup, gave thanks and offered it to them, saying, "Drink from it, all of you. This is my blood of the covenant, which is poured out for many for the forgiveness of sins. I tell you, I will not drink of this fruit of the vine from now on until that day when I drink it anew with you in my Father's kingdom." (Matt.26:27-29)

The Passover table setting contained 4 silver cups. The Four Cups the Hebrew teachers say, represented the four expressions of deliverance promised by God in Exodus chapter six and verses six and seven: "I will bring you out," "I will deliver," "I will redeem," and "I will take."

Three of the silver cups were filled with wine and one was turned down, or left empty. If this was the custom, then of course the Lord Jesus observed this practice using these four silver cups as well.

The first Cup—was the cup of *Sanctification.*"

The Second Cup—was the cup of *Deliverance.* "I will deliver you from their bondage"

The third Cup—this was the cup of *Redemption.* "I also redeem you with an out stretched arm and with great Judgment." This most possibly was the cup the Lord Jesus used when He said *"This is my blood of the covenant, which is poured out for many for the forgiveness of sins."* (Matt. 26:28)

The Cup of Redemption is also called the cup of blessing. It is a celebration of God's promise that He will redeem us. The Jews use this cup to symbolize the blood of the Passover Lamb. How significant that this is where Jesus said, "This cup is the new covenant in My blood, which is shed for you."

We must never forget that our salvation was purchased by our Lord's sacrifice on the cross. God redeemed His elect with His outstretched arm. Even so have we been redeemed by His out stretched arm upon the cross of Calvary.

Hebrews chapter nine verse twenty two tells us that without the shedding of blood there is no remission of sin.

Prophet Isaiah prophesied of the Messiah saying: *"But he was wounded for our transgressions; he was crushed for our iniquities; upon him was the chastisement that brought us peace, and with his stripes we are healed. All we like sheep have gone astray; we have turned— every one—to his own way; and the LORD has laid on him the iniquity of us all." (Isaiah 53:5-6 ESV)*

In Jesus' death, God did not just cover sin, He took it away! Anyone who places their trust in Jesus and His finished work of redemption accomplished on the cross, is passed from death due to sin, into life which is eternal. Let us remember Jesus' shed blood and the redemption He purchased for us.

The fourth cup: The Cup of *Praise or Restoration* takes place during the Hallel. This is a recitation of Psalm 136:1-16 it reads:

Give thanks to the LORD, for he is good, for his steadfast love endures forever. Give thanks to the God of gods, for his steadfast love endures forever. Give thanks to the Lord of lords, for his steadfast love endures forever; to him who alone does great wonders, for his steadfast love endures forever; to him who by understanding made the heavens, for his steadfast love endures forever; to him who spread out the earth above the waters, for his steadfast love endures forever; to him who made the great lights, for his steadfast love endures forever; the sun to rule over the day, for his steadfast love endures forever; the moon and stars to rule over the night, for his steadfast love endures forever; to him who struck down the firstborn of Egypt, for his steadfast love endures forever; and brought Israel out from among them, for his steadfast love endures forever; with a strong hand and an outstretched arm, for his steadfast love endures forever; to him who divided the Red Sea in two, for his steadfast love endures forever; and made Israel pass through the midst of it, for his steadfast love endures forever; but overthrew Pharaoh and his host in the Red Sea, for his steadfast love endures forever; to him who led his people through the wilderness, for his steadfast love endures forever; (Psalms 136:1-16 ESV)

The fourth Cup was also considered as the cup of *hope* or the *cup of Elijah.* "I will take you to myself."

These were also the words used by the Lord Jesus. What He said were the same as was said in a Jewish marriage ceremony. It was the custom of the groom after he had paid the brides price to her father. Just prior to his departure, to say to her "I go to prepare a place for you . . . ." (John 14:1-4.). The marriage was not yet final. No consummation can take place. Absolutely no sexual relationship is permitted during this time. The bride continued to live at her parents' home, separated, consecrated and set apart, for her groom. As we have already seen in the chapters dedicated to the "Ancient Jewish Wedding Customs". This is the blessed hope we have in our Lord Yeshua. His promise "I will take you unto myself".

I believe that the 4th cup is the cup of the wedding feast of the Lamb. For our Lord Yeshua said . . . *"I will not drink of this fruit of the vine until I drink it anew with you in My Father's Kingdom"* (Matt 26:29)

This tells us a couple of things. First, that there is yet another cup to be drunk. Also it tells us what that remaining cup is—the cup of the wedding feast. The Lord, in like manner and observance did not drink the 4th cup, or the cup of Elijah. This He will drink when we are all gathered with Him in the Father's Kingdom according as He has said it in verse twenty nine.

Verse thirty says that when they had sung a hymn, they went out to the Mount of Olives. It was customary for those gathered at the Passover supper to sing hymns. These Hymns were called Hallelujah songs. They were Psalms 113-115 and 118. This was exactly how the Lord Jesus' Passover Feast ended. With the giving of praises unto God the Father!

It was during Supper that the Lord Yeshua [Jesus] announced to His disciples that one of them would betray Him. In other words he was chosen for the slaughter. (Matt. 26:21-25). Notice verse 26: "And as they were eating, Jesus took bread, blessed it and broke it, and gave it to the disciples and said, 'Take, eat; this is My body.' So from that moment the unleavened bread eaten in the Old Testament Passover was to take on new significance for the disciples and the New Testament Church.

Undeniably Christ's body was to become a sacrificial offering for sin. "We have been sanctified *through the offering of the body of Jesus Christ* once for all."(Heb.10:10) It is very significant that we the Church of Yeshua understand that the significance of the observance "Passover" is now Jesus Christ the Passover Lamb. We—the church do not commemorate the deliverance of Israel from Egypt, but that of the Lord Jesus having delivered us from sin. Our observance is in remembrance of Him. "Do this in remembrance of me." (Matt. 26: 26-28; Mark 14: 22-24; Luke 22: 17-20)

Passover in the Old Testament foreshadowed The Christ Jesus' crucifixion. The New Testament Passover is a memorial of The Lord's crucifixion. By observing it, we do *"proclaim the Lord's death till He comes" (1 Cor. 11:26).* We are celebrating His death, burial and resurrection; His triumph over sin and death. Jesus is our "Passover"!

Feast of First Fruits

After the Israelites were freed from Pharaoh and Egypt, and brought to Sinai. God commanded that, after they entered the land which He had promised to them, they should hold a feast unto Him, to commemorate His goodness towards them in that land. This day would be the "Feast of First fruits" (Lev. 23:9-14). They were to offer to God the first grain (usually barley) of the first spring harvest. This was to take place during the week of the Feast of Unleavened Bread on the day after the regular weekly Sabbath. This always occurred on the first day of the week (or, more specifically, our sunset Saturday to sunset Sunday). (Tedmongomery.com/ Hebrew spring festivals/holy feast)

Yeshua is the Substance of this feast. He is the "First Fruit" It was on the first day of the week, specifically 17 day of Aviv, after Passover, angels and men alike were gathered to the tomb of Jesus, [Yeshua] and found that His body was not in the tomb. The Stone was rolled from its place at the entrance to the tomb. His burial clothes were neatly folded in the place where His body laid.

Not only was Jesus' dead body absent from the scene, but also the frightened guards were gone; gone to report that His body had disappeared—missing from the much secured tomb, and they had no idea who took him or whence was he transported to. (Luke 24:4, Matt. 28:2, 28:4). The bible says that the women came to His tomb to anoint His body with oils and spices (Mark 16:1, 2; Luke 24:1). Finding the stone rolled away (Mark 16:4; Luke 24:2), they entered and saw an angel sitting to the side (Mark 16:5). Not seeing the body of Jesus, they wondered where it might be; but the angels stood beside the women and asked, ***"Why do you look for the living among the dead? He is not here; he has risen!"*** (Luke 24:3-6a). Indeed, Jesus had risen from the dead and had left the tomb prior to sunrise that morning. Jesus made physical, flesh-and-bones appearance to well over five hundred people after He was resurrected (1 Cor. 15:5-7).

Christ was not the first person ever to be raised from the dead, no, but all the others died another death; they died a second time, but our Lord Yeshua the Resurrection and the Life; lives forevermore, He, our "Passover" is also become for us the "First Fruit".

Paul said, "But Christ has indeed been raised from the dead, the firstfruit of those who have fallen asleep. . . . For as in Adam all die, so in Christ all will be made alive. But each in his own turn: Christ, the firstfruit, then, when he comes, those who belong to him." (1 Cor. 15:20, 22, 23).

This is a glorious miracle; not that Christ rose from the dead, but rather that all who will believe in Him shall be also raised, even as the "First Fruit" has been raised unto immortality.

Feast of Unleavened Bread

When God freed Israel from slavery in Egypt, He told His people that for "seven days you shall eat unleavened bread" (Ex.12:15). Verse thirty nine further explains:

"And they baked unleavened cakes of the dough which they had brought out of Egypt; for it was not leavened, because they were driven out of Egypt and could not wait, nor had they prepared provisions for themselves."

The leavening process or the raising of the dough takes time; The Israelites had no time to wait for the dough to rise on the night when they left Egypt, so they baked and ate flat bread. What was a necessity for the people of God actually lasted seven days.

This observance according to Leviticus chapter twenty three and verse six, God appropriately named "Feast of unleavened Bread". This will come to be later called or referred to as the "Days of Unleavened Bread". ". . . *(Then were the days of unleavened bread.)*"(Acts 12:3)

There is an occasion mentioned in the gospels according to Mark and Matthew, of the Lord Jesus telling His disciples to beware of "leaven." "Watch out and beware of the leaven of the Pharisees and Sadducees" (Matt. 16:5-6, NASB). Mark added the leaven of Herod. "(Mk. 8:13-21)

The disciples at first assumed He spoke concerning their bread supply. But in-fact He as His practice was teaching them by the use of symbolism. He used the things and practices common to them to teach His lessons. Matthew records that He asked them saying:

"How is it that you do not understand that I did not speak to you concerning bread? But beware of the leaven of the Pharisees and Sadducees." Then the disciples "understood that He did not say to beware of the leaven of bread, but of the teaching of the Pharisees and Sadducees" (Vs. 11-12, NASB).

Leaven symbolizes sin. In this particular context it represents a secret pervasive false teaching, corruptive influence and rejection of Jesus as the Messiah.

But who are the Sadducees, Pharisees and Herod or Herodians? The Pharisees, the Herodians, and the Sadducees all held seats of authority and power. They were in positions of public and religious influence, and were in complete opposition to Christ Jesus.

Many scholars believe that the Herodians looked to Herod as the messiah. They considered him a sort of savior who would bring the Jews into unity with the Roman Empire adding certain favors to them. Jesus presenting Himself as the Messiah was a direct threat to the Herodians' efforts.

We are to be today careful of the spirit of the Herodians. There is a similar deceptive agent to come; the antichrist. Many will be deceived and will accept or look to the antichrist as "messiah." He will be a political leader as well as a false religious leader. This is the spirit of the leaven of Herod. It is the rejection of the true messiah in favor of political affiliations, and its benefit.

Beware of the leaven of the Pharisees: That is, of their false doctrine: this is elegantly so called; for it spreads in the soul, or the Church, as leaven does in meal. Luke 12:1. (Wesley's notes)

The *Sadducees* represented rationalism, unbelief, liberal thinking and worldliness.

Herod represented political corruption. The Lord is still giving us the same warning today; beware of human formalism, hypocrisy and traditionalism. Be careful of rationalism, unbelief, liberal mindedness and worldliness. Be aware of political corruption. Watch out for the deceptive subtle corruption of politicians (the religious)!

By "the leaven" of these is meant their doctrine, as appears from Matthew 16:12. The doctrines the Pharisees taught were the commandments and inventions of men, the traditions of the elders, free will, and justification by the works of the law: the doctrine of the Sadducees was, that there was no resurrection of the dead, nor angels, nor spirits: now because they sought secretly and artfully to infuse their notions into the minds of men; and which, when imbibed, spread their infection, and made men sour, morose, rigid, and ill natured, and swelled and puffed them up with pride and vanity, Christ compares them to leaven; and advises his disciples to look about them, to watch, and be on their guard, lest they should be infected with them. (Gill's exposition of the entire Bible)

The Days of Unleavened Bread remind us that with God's help we must remove and avoid all types of sin in all areas of our lives. Believe in and put all trust in Jesus the true Messiah and be purged of sin.

That is the observance of the Feast of Unleavened Bread—Putting away from us all that opposes God, sin. Like leaven which permeates the whole lump of dough, sin will spread in a person, a church or a nation, eventually overwhelming and bringing its participants into its bondage and eventually to death. Romans chapter six verse twenty three tells us that the wages of sin is death.

Whenever a least bit of sin is overlooked, where ever it is permitted; it will certainly permeate, leavening the lump. Sin will affect, it will infect the whole church or the whole family and community. (Gal. 5:9). When sin is permitted it will lead to other sins and eventually it will draw completely outside of the will and favor of the heavenly Father, and the Lord Jesus Christ.

Jesus is our true example of how to live leaven free. The broken unleavened bread is a type of His body that was broken for us. The bible says that in Him was no guile. No sin was in Him, but He became sin for us. He who knew no sin, became sin . . . all of our sins was heaped upon Him.

These Holy observances are supported and constructed upon each other. Together these feasts progressively reveal how God is actively working with human kind.

Earlier we saw Passover symbolizing Christ's giving of Himself for us, so our sins could be forgiven. Here in this chapter we see the picture of how we are to live now that our sin has been atoned. We must remove and avoid sin. The next Holy Day is last of the four Spring Feast, the "Festival of Pentecost".

The Festival of Pentecost

Pentecost is known by several names, which derive from its meaning and time of observance. Feast of Harvest is another name ascribed to this Holy Feast. (Ex. 23:16) according to Numbers 28:26 it is also representing the first—fruits and the Feast of Weeks (Ex. 34:22), with this name coming from the seven weeks plus one day (50 days in all) that are counted in determining when to celebrate this festival (Lev. 23:16). Similarly, in the New Testament, which was written in Greek, this festival is known as Pentecost (*Pentekostos* in the original Greek), which means "fiftieth". (Vine's Complete Expository Dictionary of Old and New Testament Words, "Pentecost").

Among Jews the most popular name for this festival is the Feast of Weeks, or Shavuot, in Hebrew. When celebrating this festival, many Jewish people recall one of the greatest events in history, God's revealing of the law at Mount Sinai.

But Pentecost doesn't just picture the giving of the law; it also shows through a great miracle that occurred on the first Pentecost of the early Church, how to keep the spiritual intent of God's laws.

Acts chapter two verses one to three states, "When the day of Pentecost came, they were all together in one place. Suddenly a sound like the blowing of a violent wind came from heaven and filled the whole house where they were sitting. They saw what seemed to be tongues of fire that separated and came to rest on each of them."

The law has and always will declare mankind guilty. The law in itself demands justice. But the spirit of Pentecost is grace; God's grace extended to us. The first Old Testament "Pentecost" event took place on the seventh weeks after the Passover Sabbath, a celebration of the giving of the Law at Sinai where God had consecrated His people for Himself. About 3000 were slain because of their unbelief and idolatry.

On the first New Testament "Pentecost" two centuries after the first "Pentecost" at Sinai, 3000 were saved because they believed in God's son Jesus Christ, of whom Peter preached. These were saved for their belief!

God had called Moses to the Mountain of Sinai and declared unto him: "You yourselves have seen what I did to Egypt, and how I carried you on eagles' wings and brought you to myself. Now if you obey me fully and keep my covenant, then out of all nations you will be my treasured possession. Although the whole earth is mine, you will be for me a kingdom of priests and a holy nation.' These are the words you are to speak to the Israelites" (Ex. 19, 3-6).

Fr. Pius Sammut, OCD writes: "This is where the real life of this people started. As one Rabbi says: "The real festival of freedom did not come until Shavu'ot (Weeks or Pentecost), when Israel stood before God on their wedding day, complete with a canopy (Mount Sinai), a ketubah (marriage contract), i.e. the Torah, and stipulations of the covenant which included a homeland and a Holy Temple which would serve to maintain the covenant. Even from a spiritual vantage point, although Pesach is when God wrought great miracles for the Jewish people, demonstrating His love and concern, He did not yet completely reveal how it was that we should serve Him.

It was not until we received the Torah on Shavu'ot, that spiritual liberation became a reality, for freedom is impossible without the Torah. Thus, Shavu'ot is the culmination of time between redemption promised and redemption realized. . . . . Pesach is when God promised to marry us; Shavu'ot is the marriage itself."

That day God engraved His Ten Words on tablets of stone. Why engraved and not written, ask the Rabbis?! While the written word remains external to the paper, they answer, the letters engraved become part of the stone. "The words of the Torah will one day be engraved in the very fabric of our heart, not merely embroidered there, as they are today, where they often fade or fray. They must penetrate to the deepest and innermost chambers of our identity, and in fact according to the prophets, will soon permanently."

"This is the framework of our Christian Pentecost." He continue to say, "Fifty days after the exodus of Jesus Christ from the tomb, Jesus Christ fulfilled the promise He made before His Ascension and He sent His Holy Spirit. The circumstances which surround the descent of the Holy Spirit echo very vividly the covenant of God with His people on Mount Sinai. On Mount Sinai, God revealed the Torah in booming voices that made Israel tremble. On Mount Zion, with "a sound like the rush of the wind" and "divided tongues as of fire" God gave us the Spirit which enables us to live the Good News. Rush of wind is parallel to the thunders and lightening on Mount Sinai. This wind which must have sounded like an on coming roar of a very fast moving train is actually the breath of life which in Genesis created life. The tongues of fire are similar to the torches which the people saw on Mount Sinai.

It is clear that the events in Acts are not just some unassociated miracles without rhyme or reason. When you put all of this together, you come to a very exciting conclusion, and it's the very same conclusion that Peter arrived at. "These men are not drunk, as you suppose . . . . No, this is what was spoken by the prophet Joel." (Acts 2:15). What did Joel prophesy about? The Prophet had announced that God was going to do something very special in Mount Zion. "And everyone who calls on the name of the LORD will be saved; for on Mount Zion and in Jerusalem, there will be deliverance . . ." (2, 32). If we can connect Mount Zion to Mount Sinai, we will have come full circle. See also Isaiah 2, 2-3.

"It is the Holy Spirit." In the Gospel of Luke, we see clearly that Jesus alone possesses the fullness of the Spirit. In the synagogue at Nazareth, Jesus applies to himself Isaiah's prophecy: 'The Spirit of the Lord is upon me because he has anointed me to preach good news to the poor.' The entire life and evangelizing activity of Jesus is guided by the Holy Spirit. The same Spirit comes down upon the Apostles at Pentecost, and ever after sustains the Church's mission. St. Paul, in his Letters, shows that the Holy Spirit is the source of the new and eternal life which Jesus communicates to his Church. The Spirit gives rise to faith, guides the prayer of Christians, and pours charity into our hearts. For St. John, on the other hand, the Spirit helps the faithful to deeply grasp the truth revealed by Christ. The Spirit is the Paraclete, the Consoler: He defends the cause of Christ, frees us from the sin which separates us from God and helps us to recognize the justice of the Father, who glorifies his Crucified Son in the Resurrection and Ascension" (Pope John Paul II, 1998)

Saint Cyril of Jerusalem asked, "Why did Christ call the grace of the Spirit water?" He answered thus: "Because all things are dependent on water; plants and animals have their origin in water. Water comes down from heaven as rain, and although it is always the same in itself, it produces many different effects . . . Like a dry tree which puts forth shots when watered, the soul bears the fruit of holiness when repentance has made it worthy of receiving the Holy Spirit.

The Spirit strengthens man's self-control, shows another how to help the poor, teaches another to fast and lead a life of asceticism, makes another oblivious of the needs of the body, and trains another for martyrdom.

The Spirit comes gently and makes himself known by his fragrance. He is not felt like a burden, for he is light, very light. Rays of light and knowledge stream before him as he approaches. The Spirit comes with the tenderness of a true friend and protector to save, to heal, to teach, to counsel, to strengthen, to console.

As light strikes the eyes of the man who come out of darkness into the sunshine and enables him to see clearly things he could not discern before, so light floods the soul of the man counted worthy of receiving the Holy Spirit and enables him to see things beyond the range of human vision, things hitherto undreamed of.

Is He not called the Spirit of God, the Spirit of truth who proceeds from the Father, the steadfast Spirit, the guiding Spirit? But his principal and most personal title is the Holy Spirit. To the Spirit all creatures turn in their need for sanctification . . . His breath empowers each to achieve its own natural end. The Spirit is the source of holiness.

Like the sunshine which permeates all the atmosphere, spreading over land and sea, and yet it is enjoyed by each person as though it were for him alone, so the Spirit pours forth his grace in full measure, sufficient for all, and yet is present as though exclusively to everyone who can receive him. To all creatures that share in him he gives a delight limited only by their own nature not by his ability to give!

The Spirit raises our hearts to heaven, guides the steps of the weak and brings to perfection those who are making progress. He enlightens those who have been cleansed from every stain of sin and makes them spiritual by communion with himself.

As clear, transparent substances become very bright when sunlight falls on them and shine with a new radiance, so also souls in whom the Spirit dwells, and who are enlightened by the Spirit, become spiritual themselves and a source of grace for others.

Through the Spirit we become citizens of heaven, we are admitted to the company of angels, we enter into eternal happiness and abide in God. Through the Spirit we acquire a likeness to God; indeed, we attain what is beyond our most sublime aspirations—we become God. (Saint Basil)

Saint Cyril of Alexandria also wrote of the Holy Spirit saying: "Only by the his presence within us in faith could Christ give us confidence to cry out Abba, Father, make it easy for us to grow in holiness and, through the possession of the all-powerful Spirit, fortify us against the wiles of the devil and the assaults of men.

It can easily be shown from examples both in the Old Testament and in the New that the Spirit changes those in whom he come to dwell; he so transforms them that they begin to live a completely new kind of life. Saul was told by the prophet Samuel: The Spirit of the Lord will take possession of you and you shall be changed into another man.

With the Spirit within them it is quite natural for people who had been absorbed by the things of this world to become entirely other-worldly in outlook and for cowards to become men of great courage. There can be no doubt that this is what happened to the disciples.

The Spirit accomplished the Father's will in men who had grown old in sin and gave them new life in Christ. Like parched ground which yields no harvest unless it receives moisture, we who were once like a waterless tree could never have lived and borne fruit without this abundant rainfall from above. If we are not to be scorched and made unfruitful, we need the dew of God. Since we have an accuser, we need an advocate as well. And so the Lord, in his pity for man, who had fallen into the hands of the brigands, having himself bound up his wounds and left for his care two coins bearing the royal image, entrusted him to the Holy Spirit. (Saint Irenaeus)

St. Ambrose said "the Holy Spirit is the River, and the abundant River, which according to the Hebrews flowed from Jesus in the lands, as we have received it prophesied by the mouth of Isaiah. This is the great River which flows always and never fails. And not only a river, but also one of copious stream and overflowing greatness, as also David said: "The stream of the river makes glad the city of God." . . . And let it not trouble you that either here it is said "rivers," or elsewhere "seven Spirits," for by the sanctification of these seven gifts of the Spirit, as Isaiah said, is signified the fullness of all virtue; the Spirit of wisdom and understanding, the Spirit of counsel and strength, the Spirit of knowledge and godliness, and the Spirit of the fear of God. One, then, is the River, but many the channels of the gifts of the Spirit. This River, then, goes forth from the Fount of Life.

The Spirit dwells in the Church and in the hearts of the faithful as in a temple. He prays in them and bears witness in them as their adoption as sons. By the power of the Gospel he enables the Church to become young, perpetually renews it, and leads it to complete union with its Bridegroom. (Vatican Council II)

Feast of Trumpets

The Feast of Trumpets introduces the autumn festivals—representing the culmination of the present age of man. The previous festivals constitute personal responses to the workings of God in the people He calls and chooses. But the Day of Trumpets heralds the intervention of God in the affairs of humanity. This Holy Day represents a dramatic turning point in world history.

This particular festival also marks the beginning of the third and final feast season (Ex. 23:14; Deut. 16:16), which includes the final four Holy Days of the year.

These Feast Days also portray the return of Jesus Christ to earth to establish the Kingdom of God!

The book of Revelation reveals a sequence of earth-shaking events depicted by angels sounding a series of seven trumpet blasts. The seventh angel's sounding of the last trumpet signifies that the kingdoms of this world have become the kingdoms of our Lord and of His Christ!

"The seventh angel sounded his trumpet, and there were loud voices in heaven, which said: "The kingdom of the world has become the kingdom of our Lord and of his Messiah, and he will reign for ever and ever." (Rev. 11:15).

Of all the prophecies in the Bible, this one surely heralds the most exciting news possible.

The Feast of Trumpets also marks the future fulfillment of the many Old Testament prophecies that speak of Messiah coming as a king. Prophet Isaiah speaks of Him saying, "The government will be upon His shoulder" and "of the increase of His government and peace there will be no end"

(Is. 9:6-7).

When Christ was brought before Pontius Pilate: being questioned by the governor; He stated clearly that He was King. He also answered that His Kingdom was not of this world. And that He had not come to rule at that time.

"My kingdom is not of this world," Jesus answered him saying "If My kingdom were of this world, my servants would fight, so that I should not be delivered to the Jews; but now My kingdom is not from here." Then Pilate asked Him, "Are You a king then?" Jesus answered in the affirmative: *"You say rightly that I am a king. For this cause I was born, and for this cause I have come into the world, that I should bear witness to the truth"*

(Jn. 18:36-37).

We see in the last moment the Lord had with His disciples before His ascension they were very intrigued; inquisitive minds wanted to know. Well after all everything else have happened as written and spoken by Him. So tell us, they asked; when would you establish the Kingdom? His reply to their question was that, it was not for them to know times or seasons which the Father has put in His own authority. (Acts 1:7). He instead told them to focus on spreading the gospel throughout the world.

Ancient Israel celebrated this Feast Day with "a sacred assembly commemorated with trumpet blasts" (Lev. 23:24). The significance of blowing the Trumpet as God had instructed ancient Israel, was to communicate essential messages: The sounding of one trumpet meant a meeting of the leaders of Israel. Two trumpets sounded to call a gathering of all of the people (Num. 10:3-4). In Exodus Chapter nineteen and verse sixteen God used a trumpet to herald His meeting with Israel when He descended upon Mount Sinai.

Trumpets could also serve for the purpose of sounding a warning. Numbers chapter 10 and verse nine states, "When you go to war in your land against the enemy who oppresses you, then you shall sound an alarm with the trumpets." In this case the trumpets resounded a warning of impending danger and imminent warfare.

Trumpets could also furnish a festive sound: *"Also in the day of your gladness, in your appointed feasts, and at the beginning of your months, you shall blow the trumpets . . . and they shall be a memorial for you before your God"* (Num. 10:10).

Psalm chapter 81 and verse 3 commands: "Blow the trumpet at the time of the New Moon, at the full moon, on our solemn feast day."

The Apostle Paul's describes for us the return of the Lord Jesus; he says "For the Lord Himself will descend from heaven with a shout, with the voice of an archangel, and *with the trumpet of God. And the dead in Christ will rise first. Then we who are alive and remain shall be caught up together with them in the clouds to meet the Lord in the air" (1 Thess. 4:16-17). This does make it very relevant, as it depicts for us the heralding of the coming of the Lord Jesus.

Paul also in First Corinthians chapter fifteen and verse fifty two speaks of the day when the first—fruits pictured by Pentecost, will be resurrected to immortal life. He says this will happen: "in a moment, in the twinkling of an eye, at the last trumpet.

For the trumpet will sound, and the dead will be raised incorruptible, and we shall be changed."

These passages noticeably demonstrate for us the significance of the Feast of Trumpets.

Feast of Atonement

We have already seen through the symbolism involved in the Passover—that Christ's shed blood atones for our sins. In fact, atonement means reconciliation.

The Day of Atonement symbolizes the reconciliation of God and all humanity.

The Day of Atonement and Passover both teach us about the forgiveness of sin and our reconciliation with God through Christ's sacrifice.

Atonement is the removal of Sin's cause and reconciliation to God.

It involves not only the forgiveness of sin; but pictures the removal of the primary cause of sin, Satan.

If we are reconciled to God through Christ's sacrifice, why do we need another Holy Day to teach us about reconciliation?

If we are already reconciled, why do we need to fast, as commanded on the Day of Atonement?

(Lev. 23:27; Acts 27:9)

What is this day's specific significance in God's master plan for the salvation of mankind?

The Day of Atonement and Passover both teach us about the forgiveness of sin and our reconciliation with God through Christ's sacrifice. However, Passover concerns the redemption of the firstborn and thus applies most directly to Christians whom God has called in this dispensation, while Atonement carries *universal* implications.

Moreover, the Day of Atonement pictures an essential additional step in God's salvation plan not found in the symbolism of the Passover.

This step must take place before humanity can experience true peace on earth.

All people are suffering the tragic consequences of sin. But sin doesn't happen without a cause, and God makes this cause clear in the symbolism associated with the Day of Atonement which involves not only the forgiveness of sin; it pictures the removal of the primary cause of sin—Satan and his demons.

Until God removes the original instigator of sin, mankind will simply continue to fall back into disobedience and suffering. Although our human nature has a part to play in our sins, Satan the devil bears great responsibility for influencing mankind to disobey God.

Even though many people doubt the existence of a devil, the Bible reveals Satan as a powerful, invisible being who can sway all man-kind. Revelation chapter twelve and verse nine tells us that his influence is so great that he *"deceives the whole world."*

The devil blinds the minds of people to the understanding of God's truth. The apostle Paul explained this in second Corinthians chapter four and verse four: "If our gospel is veiled, it is veiled to those who are perishing, whose minds *the god of this age* has blinded, who do not believe, lest the light of the gospel of the glory of Christ, who is the image of God, should shine on them" (2 Cor.4:3-4).

Paul also teaches us that Satan has influenced every human being to walk in the ways of disobedience. He notes that those called into God's Church "once walked according to the course of this world, according to *the prince of the power of the air,* the spirit who now works in the sons of disobedience"

(Eph. 2:2).

He also warned the Corinthians that Satan can present himself as righteous to lead people astray: "For Satan himself transforms himself into an angel of light. Therefore it is no great thing if his ministers also transform themselves into ministers of righteousness, whose end will be according to their works"

(2 Cor. 11:14-15).

The Lord Jesus Christ plainly stated that Satan introduced sin and rebellion into the world. To those who stood opposed to His teachings the Lord Jesus Christ declared to them saying:"

You are of your father the devil, and the desires of your father you want to do. *He was a murderer from the beginning,* and does not stand in the truth, because there is no truth in him. When he speaks a lie, he speaks from his own resources, for *he is a liar and the father of it."* (Jn. 8:44)

Tying these scriptures together allows us to see the power and the influence of Satan. Paul warned us to beware of the deceitful methods of the devil: "But I am afraid that just as Eve was deceived by the serpent's cunning; your minds may somehow be led astray from your sincere and pure devotion to Christ." (2 Cor. 11:3)

Christians who struggle to resist Satan and stop sinning fight a *spiritual battle* against the devil and his demons. Paul the Apostle explains it to us. He says in Ephesians six verses twelve, "For our struggle is not against flesh and blood, but against the rulers, against the powers, against the world forces of this darkness, against the *spiritual forces of wickedness"*

He further explains that the Lord Jesus will deliver us from the influence of the devil (vs. 13-18). Most certainly, God is much more powerful than Satan, but we must do our part by *actively resisting* the devil and the desires of the flesh. (Jas 4:7)

The Day of Atonement looks forward to the time during which Satan's deception will be removed and he will no longer be free to influence and deceive mankind. This is the time when he will be cast in to the lake of fire, prepared for him and his angels. (Rev. 20:1-3)

Feast of Tabernacles

I said before that if we the church had a better understanding of the Holy Days or Feast Days we would have a greater understanding of Scriptures all together. We might be better able to understand and to interpret the scriptures in their context.

Let us consider for a moment when Jesus took the disciples up on the mount of transfiguration, in particular the words spoken by the Apostle Peter. "Lord let us build here three tabernacles . . ." (Mt.17:4) I believe that this may have been in direct reference to the up coming "feast of Tabernacles" and the preparations necessary for the feast. That the Apostle thought there was not sufficient time for them to return home and to build their temporary dwelling for this Feast. His, I believe to have been nothing but, a mere suggestion to aide in their observance of the feast; in a thorough and timely fashion.

Feast of Tabernacle or "Sukkot" is agricultural in origin. This is evident from the biblical name "The Feast of Ingathering," from the ceremonies accompanying it, from the season—"The festival of the seventh month"—and occasion of its celebration: "At the end of the year when you gather in your labors out of the field" (Ex. 23:16); by its designation as "the Feast of the Lord" or simply "the Feast". Perhaps because of its wide attendance, Sukkot became the appropriate time for important state ceremonies. (Wikipedia.org)

In Leviticus, God told Moses to command the people: "On the first day you shall take the product of hadar trees, branches of palm trees, boughs of leafy trees, and willows of the brook" (Lev. 23:40), and "You shall live in booths seven days; all citizens in Israel shall live in booths, in order that future generations may know that I made the Israelite people live in booths when I brought them out of the land of Egypt" (Lev. 23:42-43).

Feast of Tabernacles, Feast of Booths or Sukkot is a seven day observance, with the first day celebrated as a full festival with special prayer services and holiday meals. The remaining days are known as Chol HaMoed ("festival weekdays"). The seventh day of Sukkot is called Hoshana Rabbah ("Great Hoshana", referring to the tradition that worshippers in the synagogue walk around the perimeter of the sanctuary during morning services) and has a special observance of its own. Outside Israel, the first two days are celebrated as full festivals. Throughout the week of Sukkot, meals are eaten in the sukkah and Orthodox Jewish families sleep there, although the requirement is waived in case of rain. Every day, a blessing is recited over the Lulav and the Etrog. Observance of Sukkot is detailed in the Book of Nehemiah in the Bible, the Mishnah(Sukkah 1:1-5:8); the Tosefta (Sukkah 1:1-4:28); and the Jerusalem Talmud (Sukkah 1a-) and Babylonian Talmud(Sukkah 2a-56b).

The Feast of Tabernacles or Sukkot, symbolizes God's plan of restoration for mankind. Apostle Peter after having received the Holy Spirit He preached:

"Repent therefore and be converted, that your sins may be blotted out, so that times of refreshing may come from the presence of the Lord, and that He may send Jesus Christ, who was preached to you before, whom heaven must receive until the times of restoration of all things, which God has spoken by the mouth of all His holy prophets since the world began" (Acts 3:19-21).

What are these "times of refreshing" and "times of restoration" of which Peter spoke of? They are the "restoration" process which will start with the return of Jesus Christ, pictured by the Feast of Trumpets, and the banishment of Satan, depicted by the Day of Atonement.

Once these events have taken place, as represented by the previous Holy Days, the foundation is in place for the restoration of the creation to peace and harmony with God.

This Feast also reflects the "rest" symbolized by the weekly Sabbath: *"Let us, therefore, make every effort to enter that rest, so that no one will perish by following their example of disobedience." (Heb.4:1-11) this is the celebration of the great harvest of humanity.* (Is. 11:9-10).

It was God's plan and desire to enjoy fellowship with mankind. But the sin, disobedience of man, caused a breach in that relationship. Well He had a plan to remedy that, foreshadowed in all these Holy Days. All will be as the LORD desires, as in the beginning. God will look at His creation and will say as He did at the first, "It is good" (Gen. 1:31).

There shall be times of refreshing and times of restoration. God and his man together for all eternity!

Through one man [Adam] sin entered the world, and death through sin, and thus death spread to all men, because all sinned . . ." (Rom. 5:12). Remedial action has been taken; God gave His only begotten Son. The second Adam, Yeshua the Christ. That by His righteousness all who believe in Him—will be made righteous.

"For since by man [Adam] came death, by Man [Christ] also came the resurrection of the dead. For as in Adam all die, even so in Christ all shall be made alive" say Apostle Paul in first Corinthians chapter fifteen, verses twenty one and twenty two.

So there we have it the "Rehearsal" as God had intricately woven into human kind's life and worship, in order to clearly offer us a perfect preview of His intended plan. Shrouded in shadows and types, all are clearly revealed in our Lord and Christ, Jesus [Yeshua]!

The Spirit of the Feast

The Lord Jesus was very vocal about the manner by which the Jewish people of His day observed these holy days. And in no way was He saying not to observe. But what He addressed was, the spirit in which these were observed.

In Mark chapter two and verse twenty seven, He spoke to those that accused Him of not keeping the Sabbath day holy: *"The Sabbath was made for man, not man for the Sabbath"* (Mk.2:27) In other words the Sabbath day is for meeting the needs of man, not man meeting the requirements of the Sabbath. Understand, the reason for their accusation was simply because he and his disciples on the Sabbath broke ears of corn to satisfy their hunger.

Notice their hearts' condition—on the very Sabbath day? Busy observing the day, yet had they no regard for the well-being of others. *"Is it such a fast that I have chosen?"* Asked the Lord in Isaiah chapter fifty eight: *"a day for a man to afflict his soul? is it to bow down his head as a bulrush, and to spread sackcloth and ashes under him? will you call this a fast, and an acceptable day to the LORD? Is not this the fast that I have chosen? to loose the bands of wickedness, to undo the heavy burdens, and to let the oppressed go free, and that you break every yoke? Is it not to deal your bread to the hungry, and that you bring the poor that are cast out to your house? When you see the naked, that you cover him; and that you hide not yourself from your own flesh? . . ."*

There is more to the observance than the rituals. The heart must be right; a contrite and a broken heart the Lord will not despise.

The leaders in the temple on the Sabbath when Jesus healed the woman that was bowed over for 18 years. They too had a heart problem. The Lord was so disgusted by their hypocrisy; He said to them: "You loosed your asses and give them water. But this woman a daughter of Abraham you would deny her from being loosed!" (Lk.13:15-16

In regards to the how of these observances, and as to the spirit of the Feast; Apostle

Paul instructs in his letter to the Colossians, chapter two, verses fifteen to seventeen: ". . . And having spoiled principalities and powers, he made a show of them openly, triumphing over them in it. Let no man therefore judge you in meat, or in drink, or in respect of an holy day, or of the new moon, or of the Sabbath days: *Which are a shadow of things to come; but the body is of Christ.*" To the church in Rome he wrote saying: 'The one who eats everything must not treat with contempt the one who does not, and the one who does not eat everything must not judge the one who does, *for God has accepted them.*" (Rom. 14:3)

He continues in verses 5, "One person considers one day more sacred than another; another considers every day alike. *Each of them should be fully convinced in their own mind.*"

This I propose also, "For the kingdom of God is not a matter of eating and drinking, *but of righteousness, peace and joy in the Holy Spirit,* "(vs. 17).

Since you died with Christ to the elemental spiritual forces of this world, why, as though you still belonged to the world, do you submit to its rules: (Col. 2:20)." Remember whom Paul was speaking to; these were converted pagan worshipers (Gentiles), who were turning back to their old ways, practices and customs. He was not telling his readers not to keep the Holy Feast, rather he was refuting others judgements of them for observing the holy days. And their turning back to the old pagan worship.

I beg of you Bride of Yeshua, [Saints of God] do not any longer partake of the things which are offered to idols. Cease from pleasing men, instead please God. Stop being tossed to and fro by all sorts of doctrine. And be holy even as your God is holy.

Separate yourselves as the dear elect, chosen of God to show forth His glory and praise. We are the bride of Christ, purchased by His precious blood. Therefore let us be possessed with the mind of Christ. Who, being in very nature God, did not consider equality with God something to be used to his own advantage; rather, he made himself nothing by taking the very nature of a servant being made in human likeness. And being found in appearance as a man, he humbled himself by becoming obedient to death—even death on a cross! (Phil.2:1-11)

This is the spirit of the Bride of Jesus Christ: A heart that loves God, consecrated unto Him, and completely humbled to do what He commands. The sacrifice is worthy and accepted by God because the worshipper is obedient to Him. It is the heart that God takes notice of. *Man looks at the outward appearances. What is done outwardly, but God looks at the heart.*

"Obedience is better than sacrifice."(1Sam. 15:22-23)

In this text, Saul had chosen to do what he thought was right in his own eyes. And completely disregarded what the Lord had commanded him to do. It does not matter how much we are offering, giving or doing to God, if we do so in disobedience God will have no respect for what we do, He will reject it.

The spirit of obedience validates the sacrifice. In Hosea chapter six and verse six, the Lord speaks to wanton Israel—*"I delight in loyalty rather than sacrifice."*

It does not worth a thing, and God is certainly not impressed. Unless what we do is done from a spirit of Love, humility and obedience to our Heavenly Father, we are wasting our time. It is not because your grandmother did it, or what you have heard all your life. Traditions that are born of stubbornness is witchcraft, it is sin! It is entirely because the Heavenly Father commands it. As imitators of Jesus our Lord we do as He Had done, It is purely because the Heavenly Father commands it; *that which the Father say and do!*

Conclusion

Remember that "festival" or "feasts," in Hebrew, is *hag* or *mo'ed*, a "set time" or "appointed time." An appointed festival or feast is a "holy convocation" or "sacred assembly," meaning in Hebrew *mikrah*, a "rehearsal" or a "recital." Therefore, for Jews and non-Jews alike, all of the festivals and feasts appointed by God as "rehearsals" are for the purpose of revealing the Messiah (Col. 2:16, 17) and completing God's overall Plan. They were shadows cast before that which was to come; the substance—Jesus Christ the Lord.

The Spring Feasts—represented Christ' life (Fulfilled)
Pass Over—Jesus' Death
Unleavened—His Burial
First Fruit—His Resurrection
Pentecost—The coming of the Holy Spirit
The Fall Feasts: Jesus' last coming

The feast of Trumpets, Tabernacles and Day of Atonement are fulfilled during Christ return. These three Hebraic feasts/ festivals/holy days, which take place in the Fall of the year, represent events in the second (latter) Coming of the Messiah. They also are known as the "latter rain" festivals. Yeshua [Jesus], as the conquering, judging, ruling King, will be the personal fulfillment of these festivals/holy days in their full significance. (tedmontgomery. com)

All of Gods Feasts are depictions of that which He had accomplished and is working for our benefit. They are symbolisms and representation of the Christ, the son of God. When the substance [Christ] is made manifest, the types and shadows are over-come by Him [Christ] and brought to an end.

I know you have a question; and that is— so should Christians observe these Holy Days? It is important for us, Christians not to base our Passover observance on the Exodus or Deuteronomy administrations, but to follow Christ's instructions as the Passover Lamb and High Priest of a better covenant.

The Exodus, Deuteronomy and New Covenant Passovers all reflect God working out His plan of salvation. Each administration involves different ways of celebrating both the temporary realities of the people of those times and the future reality when Jesus Christ would become the Passover and administer the New Covenant as the High Priest of God.

Christ has left a clear example of how the New Covenant Passover is to be observed. As the apostle Paul wrote, "For I received from the Lord that which I also delivered to you: that the Lord Jesus on the same night in which He was betrayed took bread; and when He had given thanks, He broke it and said, 'Take, eat; this is My body which is broken for you; do this in remembrance of Me.' In the same manner He also took the cup after supper, saying, 'This cup is the new covenant in My blood. This do, as often as you drink it, in remembrance of Me.' for as often as you eat this bread and drink this cup, you proclaim the Lord's death till He comes" (1 Cor. 11:23-26)

An enlightening article by Robert Somerville, reads: "Now let us establish some proper motivational factors. Our celebration of the Biblical memorial days are not a matter of salvation or acceptance before God. Therefore our motive in celebration should be as God originally intended; remembrance and honor for what He has done. God said his feasts were to be celebrated "forever" (Ex. 12:14, Lev. 23:21, Lev. 23:41). If God never changes, and we have His word on that He does not (Mal. 3:6), it is obvious that He still desires to be worshiped in this manner. The feast days retain a deep abiding meaning for the Christian since their fullness (not termination) is found in Jesus the Messiah.

It is safe to say that the Christian has as much reason for celebrating these festivals as does the Jew and perhaps more (1 Cor. 5:8).

The feast days contain more divine information, spiritual lessons and prophetic reflections than perhaps any subject of scripture. Subsequently, it is through our deliberate recognition and celebration of them that the riches of truth contained in them is released for our understanding.

The things that are done to celebrate these days are not so important as the acknowledgement of the day itself. We need not be concerned with ancient ritualism from which we were liberated in Christ (Heb. 9:10) but focus on the basic principle of their prophetic and spiritual meaning as is revealed under the New Covenant. Since it is not a matter of salvation but one of worship, there is liberty and flexibility in what we can do as a remembrance practice. The spirit of praise and worship simply demands the recognition of the Biblical feast days. No other conclusion can be drawn.

The question before us is; should Christians celebrate the feast days? Clearly we should. Why? Because they are Biblical, Christ-centered and God ordained. While feast celebrations may not be essential to salvation, they are certainly essential for a more perfect worship order in the church. Reason simply dictates this conclusion. (Read further books or articles by Robert Somerville, awarenessministry.org)

My conclusion on the subject of keeping the Old Testament feast is simply this, "Let us keep the Feast" as says Apostle Paul.

The feast of trumpets are ahead of us when the Lord the Substance shall again be seen. The promise of Pentecost is already come so we are to observe daily. It is not by might nor by power but by the Spirit of the Lord. We need the comfort, teaching and guidance of the Holy Spirit all the time. We need His love, wisdom, will, strength and empowerment that only come through Holy Spirit. Let us worship God the way He has commanded us to.

God will not accept sacrifice offered on a pagan alter! We seem to be of the opinion that it is okay to celebrate these "holidays" as long as we do so in the name of Jesus. "You worship" said the Lord Jesus: "and know not what you worship"

Eusebius (A.D. 263-339) gives us a glimpse into the early church in *The History of the Church*. He records that in the early second century a bishop from Asia Minor named Polycarp confronted the bishop of Rome over the issue of observing the Passover on Abib 14 instead of celebrating Easter. Polycarp claimed to have been a disciple of the apostle John and taught that the Passover was the true observance of the apostles.

In the latter half of the second century the Passover controversy became critical and divided the churches in Asia Minor from those who observed Easter in the West. The Passover contingents, known as Quartodecimans, were led by Polycrates. In a letter to the bishop in Rome, Polycrates wrote, "We for our part keep the day scrupulously, without addition or subtraction. For in Asia great luminaries sleep who shall rise again on the day of the Lord's advent, when He is coming in glory from heaven and shall search out all the saints . . . All of these kept the fourteenth day of the month as the beginning of the Paschal festival, in accordance with the Gospel, not deviating in the least but following the rule of the Faith" (*The History of the Church*, Eusebius, pages 230-231).

Most of these "holidays", are born out of Satan's deception and the stubbornness of man's heart. Their origins are deeply rooted in paganism; the worship of false gods. Easter was never even an observance of the early church or the Apostles of Jesus.

The only place in the bible where we will find any direct mention of "Easter" is in Acts chapter twelve verse four, and this was in reference to the pagan celebration which was just after the Passover (Observed by Jesus and the Apostle) and perhaps during the feast of Unleavened Bread (Observed by Jesus and the Apostles).

The Lord Jesus has left a clear example for us to follow; may we so follow His teachings, His doctrines even as the Apostles did. *"They continued in the Apostles doctrine . . . ."* (Acts 2:42) their customs were that of teaching, prayer and breaking of bread. Partaking of the death and suffering of Jesus Christ.

The times and seasons of the Holy Days and Feast of God are associated with the fulfillment of divine prophesies.

It was during a celebration in Jerusalem that the Passover was fulfilled in the Messiah becoming as the Servant of God the Passover Lamb; whose blood was sprinkled before His heavenly Father on the mercy seat.

Also during a celebration in Jerusalem that Pentecost or the Feast of Weeks was fulfilled. The Holy Spirit, the Comforter, was poured out on the early believers.

It was during the Feast of Tabernacles that the Lord Jesus made His wonderful promise of rivers of living water! The Lord Jesus made this offer during the last and great day of the Feast of Tabernacles, thus indicating that the wonderful day during which the Lord would give us the former and latter rains would be during the Feast of Tabernacles. These Fall Feasts: Trumpets, Tabernacles and Day of Atonement; are of most significance to us, as they are yet to be fulfilled. Be watchful, observing the feast of God—His "Rehearsals"

Church, the Lord's coming is nearer than we think, it is eminent. I beseech you to be watchful, redeeming the times. Be ready for His appearing, He is coming! Be ready and waiting, for in such a moment that ye think not the Son of man cometh.

"For the Lord himself shall descend from heaven with a shout, with the voice of the archangel, and with the trump of God: and the dead in Christ shall rise first: Then we which are alive and remain shall be caught up together with them in the clouds, to meet the Lord in the air: and so shall we ever be with the Lord." (1Thess.4:16, 17) And this is still not the climax as yet!

But it is as the Prophets prophesy, and is stated in Revelation chapter twenty: when the devil and his demons would be finally bound and cast into the lake of fire and be tormented day and night for ever and ever. And there shall be a recreation of all things in earth, and the lion shall lie down with the lamb. All will be peace and joy forever more. Just as our Father in Heaven intended and purposed for us.

We shall live and reign with Him forever and ever. His glory will be light for us so there will be no need for the sun. Praise God! There will be no more pain; no more sorrow; no dying and all will be peace for ever more. Praise God forever!

God through the apostle John, has shown us the picture of the beginning of all things perfect; he said: "Then the Angel showed me Water-of-Life River, crystal bright. It flowed from the Throne of God and the Lamb, right down the middle of the street. The Tree of Life was planted on each side of the River, producing twelve kinds of fruit, a ripe fruit each month. The leaves of the Tree are for healing the nations. Never again will anything be cursed.

The Throne of God and of the Lamb is at the center. His servants will offer God service—worshiping, they'll look on his face, their foreheads mirroring God. Never again will there be any night. No one will need lamplight or sunlight. The shining of God, the Master, is all the light anyone needs. And they will rule with Him age after age after age. (Rev. 22:1-5 Message Bible)

Wow! This is the destiny of the Bride of Christ Yeshua [Jesus]. "Eye has not seen, nor ear heard, Nor have entered into the heart of man The things which God has prepared for those who love Him." (1Cor.2:9)

Edwards Brothers Malloy
Oxnard, CA USA
September 5, 2014